IN PURSUIT OF A BETTER LIFE

IN PURSUIT OF A BETTER LIFE

How to Create a Successful and Fulfilling Life

BENJAMIN M. NOYNAY

BMN Publishing

Copyright © 2022 Benjamin M. Noynay

Published in Australia by: BMN Publishing
Cover and Interior design by: Benjamin M. Noynay

All rights reserved. No part of this book may be reproduced by any mechanical, photographic, or electronic process, or in the form of a phonographic recording; nor may it be stored in a retrieval system, transmitted, or otherwise be copied for public or private use—other than for "fair use" as brief quotations embodied in articles and reviews—without prior written permission of the publisher.

The Author/Publisher has strived to be as accurate and complete as possible in the creation of this book, notwithstanding the fact that he does not warrant or represent at any time that the contents within are accurate due to the rapidly changing nature of the Internet. This book is a common-sense guide to pursuing success. In practical advice books, like anything else in life, there are no guarantees of income made. Readers are cautioned to reply on their own judgment about their individual circumstances and to act accordingly. This book is not intended for use as a source of legal, business, accounting, or financial advice. All readers are advised to seek the services of competent professionals in the legal, business, accounting, and finance fields.

Cataloging-in-Publication Data is on file at the National Library of Australia
ISBN: 978-0-6456085-0-2
e-book ISBN: 978-0-6456085-1-9

10 9 8 7 6 5 4 3 2 1
First Printing 2022

Printed in Australia by Lightning Source Printing Company

For my parents, Ruperto Noynay and Eligia Montealto, who not only taught me but most of all showed me, in their own way, what I needed to know to pursue a better life.

For my wife, Sonia, and three children and their families, Benson & Erin, Simon, and Maryson & Nathaniel, and two granddaughters, Diana Grace Noynay and River Eve Douglas, for being my reasons to pursue a better life.

CONTENTS

dedication   v
Introduction   xi

SECTION ONE
THE RIGHT ATTITUDE TO LEARNING   **1**

  1 The Four Stages of Learning   3

  2 What Are You Learning?   9

  3 How Are You Learning?   13

  4 Learning from the Experts   25

  5 The Three Conditions for Learning   57

SECTION TWO
SETTING S.M.A.R.T. GOALS   **63**

  6 What Is Your Dream in Life?   65

  7 What Are SMART Goals?   69

  8 Are You Aiming for Prosperity?   73

  9 To Go or Not to Go?   77

| 10 | Is Having a Dream Enough to Succeed? | 81 |

SECTION THREE
DETERMINATION AND PERSISTENCE — 87

11	Determination and Persistence	89
12	Work Smarter, Not Harder	93
13	The Cycle of Success	99
14	The Three Levels of Commitment	107
15	The Principle of Self-Discipline	115

SECTION FOUR
LEVELS OF EXCELLENCE — 119

16	The Secret of Fulfillment is Excellence	121
17	Understanding and Overcoming the Fear of Failure	129
18	The Ladder to Excellence	137
19	The Best Pathway To Success	145
20	Maximizing Your God-Given Gifts	153

SECTION FIVE
THE MISSIONS OF LEADERSHIP — 161

21	The RIGHT Principles to Live By	163
22	The Joy of Living Is in Giving	171
23	The Principle of Empowerment	179

24	Leadership Is Action, Not Position	187
25	Your Abundant, Balanced, and Fulfilling Life	195
26	A.G.D.E.L. in Summary	203

Final Thoughts 207
About The Author 208

INTRODUCTION

It is natural to desire a better life, and there is a lot to consider when looking to improve the quality of your life. For example, a better life for you may be to enhance your work-life balance. This could include trying to get more time off from work or even taking a day or two off to attend to other obligations outside of work. The key is trying to find the right balance of work and relaxation.

Another way to upgrade the quality of your life is to focus on self-care. It is important that you take time to care for yourself by eating right, exercising, and nurturing your mental health. We can only do the things we want to do when we are healthy.

Many people are looking to leave their troubles behind and start anew. Think for a moment. Is this really what you are looking for, or are you searching for happiness? Happiness does not come by staying in one place forever. It comes by exploring and experiencing new things. This is what makes life fulfilling. To live a fulfilled life, you must be willing to grow and try new experiences. It doesn't matter what you do, as long as you are doing things that make you happy.

A major part of what makes people happy is their mental well-being which includes a healthy lifestyle and maintaining a positive mental attitude. One way a positive attitude can be achieved is by learning to practice the virtue of gratitude. Be thankful for what you have.

Of course, you probably realize that acquiring and possessing wealth is not the true gauge of where someone's happiness lies. If one were to perceive joy from simple things like acquiring material goods, then each person who encounters and gains it should also have a universal experience of joy, or so some may think (or do).

In life, it is not enough to be emotionally stable. People undergo changes that make seeking happiness a continual process. The natural evolution in life follows a specific path; thus, when facing objects and environments that include both contradictory qualities, the human mind evades them to reach fulfillment. Making that change starts with one step which will shape your success for a lifetime.

In writing this book, it is my objective to teach you the guiding principles that will lead to the achievement of your goal to experience and live a successful life. Through these chapters, you will discover tools to help you find financial freedom while also pursuing the art of happiness. Kindly note that our level of joy is not necessarily directly proportional to our monetary wealth, and yet most people want both: more happiness and more prosperity.

This book is exactly what you are looking for. It delves straight into your innermost subconscious driving forces. Unlike many other textbooks on the same subject, this one will target specific areas of personal growth that I can assure you will bring a smile back onto your face. It is obvious, focused, and above anything else, readable.

Ultimately, everyone has their own idea of what constitutes success. And yet, there are some steps that can be taken to elevate the quality of your life. If you're not satisfied with the way your workday goes, try following these steps to make it better:

- Plan and take ownership of your mistakes.
- Accept responsibility for your actions.
- Be accountable for the results of your decisions.
- Focus on the quality of everything.
- Challenge yourself all the time.
- Analyze what you want to change.
- Find your inner superpower.
- Take advantage of self-talk and autosuggestion.
- Be specific about what you want in life.
- Visualize your goal every single day.
- Learn to adapt to new situations and environments.
- Believe in yourself.
- Live positively and peacefully.
- Be open-minded.
- Help others when you can.
- Encourage those around you to do the same.
- Pay it forward.

In this book, you will discover the formula I have been using over the years in my own pursuit of a better life. I call it the "AGDEL" Formula, and each ingredient is a separate section in the book:

1: The Right ATTITUDE to Learning
2: Setting Smart GOALS
3: DETERMINATION and Persistence
4: Levels of EXCELLENCE
5: The Missions of LEADERSHIP

I wish you all the best as you utilize the principles in this book in your pursuit of a better life.

Good luck.

SECTION ONE

The Right ATTITUDE to Learning

CHAPTER 1

The Four Stages of Learning

Have you ever felt overwhelmed by all there is to learn? That's exactly how I feel every time I go online. You probably experience the same thing when you browse the Internet. Perhaps, this is the reason why we feel like we don't have enough time to learn what we need to in order to achieve what we want in life. As a matter of fact, there are some people who tend to give up learning because they think they could never become good at what they're trying to study. Some people are so overwhelmed they completely shut down.

We must keep in mind that learning is a process.

Just bear in mind that whatever you are trying to master, you always start as a beginner. Then after some time, you move up to a much higher level and may call yourself an advanced learner. Then after some more time, you will reach the ranks of professionals. And there are some who pursue an even higher level that we call experts.

This whole process of learning has four stages—Unconscious Incompetence, Conscious Incompetence, Conscious Competence, and Unconscious Competence. Each of the stages has its own timeline.

Let's look more closely at these stages.

1. UNCONSCIOUS INCOMPETENCE

This is the stage where you don't know what you don't know. But you don't even know that.

Let's take an infant, for example. Obviously, an infant doesn't know how to tie a tie, and he doesn't care, simply because he doesn't know that he doesn't know how to tie a tie. He doesn't even know what a tie is. It may seem silly to think about an infant not knowing what a tie is, but you get the point.

Would you believe that there are lots of adults until now who still don't know how to tie their ties? OK, enough! So, we all start our learning from this stage. And there's nothing wrong with that. Let's move on to the next stage.

2. CONSCIOUS INCOMPETENCE

This is the stage where you know what you don't know. Being aware of what we don't know is the beginning of the most exciting journey in the world of learning or knowledge acquisition as others might call it.

For example, I know that I don't know how to play the saxophone. I know that I don't know how to fly a plane. But I don't stop there. Now that I am aware of what I don't know, it's up to me to decide whether to pursue the requisite knowledge and develop the needed skills to perform those functions or not. I now can do something about it, if I so choose. It's exciting, isn't it? If I decide to pursue such knowledge, I then move on to the third stage.

3. CONSCIOUS COMPETENCE

This is the stage where you know what you know but have to think about it first. And if you are at this level, you know how to do something, at least to some degree. We become competent only in things that we know how to do, and this is probably the most exciting point in the world of learning because now you can do what you know. However, this is also the most dangerous stage because this is where most people get stuck.

So, what happens that can make you plateau? You don't want to learn anything anymore aside from what you already know how to do. In other words, you don't want to move up to the next level because you already feel so comfortable with what you think you know how to do very well (or well enough).

Let's take playing a musical instrument, for example. Maybe you know someone who knows how to play the guitar but is never considered a *guitarist*. Or maybe you know someone who knows how to play the piano but is never considered a *pianist*. This is the reason why there are so many guitar players or piano players in the world but there are only a few guitarists or pianists. Those who are at this stage will do whatever it takes to defend what they think they know rather than opening their minds to new ways of learning or doing things. It's sad, isn't it?

If you are in this stage, get out of there and move up to the next level of learning. You can become an expert in what you think you know how to do well, which is the fourth stage of learning.

4. UNCONSCIOUS COMPETENCE

This is the stage where you know what you know automatically. When you reach this stage of learning, you don't even have to think about it. You just do it unconsciously. The skill has become a part of you; it's second nature.

The best example of this stage is driving a car. When you were learning how to drive, did you get scared? I don't know about you, but I was terrified. Although I learned to drive back in my country, the Philippines, ten years prior and I knew that I knew how to drive (that is, I was in the third stage), or so I thought.

When we migrated to Australia, I thought I knew I could drive because I'd been driving for many years. On the second day after we arrived, I drove my mother-in-law's car. It was a weird feeling having the steering wheel on the right side of the car and driving on the left side of the road, but I didn't give it much thought because I knew how to drive. Oh boy, was I wrong, big time! I almost killed myself because I was driving on the wrong side of the road.

My friend from New Zealand has wisely described my driving experience in one of his blogs when he said driving in Australia is *"as when left is right"* and *"as when right is wrong."*

After a few years, of course, I can now hold a bottle of water with my left hand, drink the water while driving a manual transmission car, and still arrive at my destination very safely. Now driving a car in Australia is second nature to me. I know what I know automatically.

I hope these four stages in learning give you hope that you can learn anything if you put your mind and heart into it. Just give yourself enough time to keep practicing. With enough diligence you will become an expert and achieve your goals in life, and possibly even inspire others along the way.

CHAPTER 2

What Are You Learning?

To learn or *not to learn*: that is no longer the question. Whether you like it or not, you are learning. The moment you were born, you started learning, and for as long as you are alive, you continue to learn. Indeed, life is a continuous learning journey. The question is, *What* are you learning?

As we keep living our lives, we keep learning so many things. It is common knowledge that life is a duality, which means in everything, there are always two sides. The good thing about this is that we can choose what we want to learn. God has endowed us with freewill so that we can select the subjects or topics we desire. So, again, what are you learning? Are you learning about yourself, about other people, and about the world around you?

The answer to these questions depends on what you pay attention to and what you choose to focus on. If you are focusing on the negative aspects of life, you will learn about pessimism, anger, hatred, and bitterness. If you are focusing on the positive aspects of life, you will learn about optimism, love, compassion, and hope. It's up to you to decide what you want to learn and what you want to focus on.

Personally, one of the things that I am learning in life is that it is important to be kind to others. This includes being kind to myself. I am learning how to be more patient, how to forgive myself and others, and how to be more compassionate. These are all important lessons that are helping me to become a more peaceful person—and I presume more pleasant to be around, too.

Another thing that I am learning is how to be happy in the present. It is not always easy to be happy when life is difficult, but I am learning that it is possible. I am also learning how to enjoy the simple things in life and to appreciate the moment for what it is. This is helping me to live a more joyful life with greater awareness.

Every day we are learning something new.

Whether it is big or small, we are constantly expanding our knowledge and growing as individuals. The things that we learn can vary greatly, but there are some common lessons that we all tend to learn at some point.

One of the most important things that we learn is how to be ourselves and love ourselves. This may sound simple, but it is quite a challenging task. We all have different personalities and different ways of looking at the world, and it can be difficult to find our place. We all must learn how to be comfortable in our own skin, and this takes time and practice.

We also often have a lot of negative thoughts about ourselves and need to learn how to let go of those thoughts and accept ourselves for who we are. Once we learn to love ourselves, we can start to love others more fully as well.

We also learn about the world beyond our personal bubbles. We learn about history, both ancient and modern, and about other cultures. We learn about the challenges they faced. We learn about the environment and how to take care of it. We learn about the economy and how it works. We learn about the world's problems and how we can help solve them.

Finally, we learn that the world is not always fair. We may experience a lot of disappointment and heartache in our lives, but we eventually learn that this is just a part of life. We learn to accept the bad with the good, and we learn to appreciate the good even more because of the bad.

These are just a few of the things that we all discover on our continuous learning journey. Life is a never-ending learning experience, and it is up to us to determine what we want to understand and know and what we want to focus on.

So, what about you? What are you learning? Every person will experience different things, and there is no one right way to learn and grow. The important thing is to keep learning and growing no matter what life throws our way.

CHAPTER 3

How Are You Learning?

To find out how you are learning and what type of learner you are, it is very important to understand the three major factors making up your learning style.

- The Three Sensory Learning Styles
- The Two Types of Reasoning
- The Two Learning Environments

1. THE THREE SENSORY LEARNING STYLES

There are three main types of sensory learners: visual, auditory, and kinesthetic. Each individual has their own unique way of acquiring knowledge and understanding new information. At the end of this chapter, I hope you shall be able to identify your own learning style and hopefully you can use it to start your journey to pursue your own version of a better life.

a. Visual Learners

Visual learners learn best when they can see what they are learning. They might prefer to watch videos or look at pictures while they are learning. They can often remember things they have seen better than what they have heard or physically touched.

There are some things that visual learners can do to help them learn better. For example, they can use flashcards with pictures on them, or draw diagrams to help them understand concepts. They can also take reinforcement breaks by looking at something new they are trying to learn and then write down what they learned each day.

Visual learners often do well in school because most classrooms use visual aids. However, it is important for visual learners to find ways to learn outside of the classroom as well, so they can continue learning throughout their lives.

Many research studies have found that about 65% of the population consists of visual learners.

---

b. *Auditory Learners*

The auditory learner is someone who learns best through listening. They might have an easier time understanding the content if they listen to a lecture rather than reading a textbook. Auditory learners often have strong memories for sounds and words. They may be able to recall information they heard days or even weeks ago. Because they learn best through listening and reciting aloud, they are usually good speakers and communicators. They often prefer verbal instructions over written instructions, and audios over videos.

An interesting note: Reading can be considered visual or auditory. If a person "hears" the words in their head or likes to read by listening to audio books, they are more auditory; otherwise, they may be more visual.

There are a few things that teachers can do to help auditory learners succeed in the classroom. First, provide verbal instructions whenever possible. Second, give students opportunities to talk and discuss the material they are learning. Third, provide listening activities such as lectures, discussions, stories, jokes, and debates. And fourth, create a classroom environment that is supportive and positive.

Auditory learners can be very successful students, but they need teachers who understand their strengths and can help them to capitalize on them. About 30% are auditory learners.

Auditory learners may need:

1. Extra time to talk through new concepts aloud.
2. A lot of verbal explanations and examples.
3. Opportunities to repeat information and practice new skills.
4. Organization and clarity in lectures and lesson plans.
5. A calm and structured learning environment.

c. Kinesthetic Learners

Kinesthetic learners learn by doing. They like to be active and use their hands and body to expand their knowledge and understand concepts in a bodily way. There are several ways to accommodate kinesthetic learners in the classroom. One way is to give them opportunities to move around.

You can have them do physical exercises or walk around the room while they are learning. Another way is to give them hands-on tasks. Have them build things, solve puzzles, create art or props, or do other activities that involve using their hands.

Kinesthetic learners often have a lot of energy, so it's important to be active when learning. They may not be good at sitting still for long periods of time.

Here are a few ideas for kinesthetic learners:

1. Do physical exercises such as jumping jacks or squats while learning.
2. Move around while speaking.
3. Use your hands and move your body when learning.
4. "Anchor" new information by touching part of your body, for example, your thigh, your forehead, or bringing your fingertips together in the OK symbol.

2. THE TWO TYPES OF REASONING

There are two types of reasoning used in learning: deductive and inductive.

a. *Deductive Reasoning*

Deductive reasoning is based on the principle that if something is true of a particular thing, it is true of all things of that kind. For example, if I know that all squares are rectangles, then I can conclude that any square is a rectangle. Deductive reasoning is often used to create proofs in mathematics.

Deductive reasoning is a key component of learning. To integrate new knowledge, we need to be able to take what we know and apply it to new situations. Deductive reasoning helps us to do this by allowing us to use our knowledge to create hypotheses and then test them. This process helps us learn not just specific facts, but also how to think critically and problem solve.

The ability to use deductive reasoning is important in all areas of life. In school, it helps us to master new subjects and understand complex concepts. In our careers, it allows us to come up with innovative solutions to problems. And in our personal lives, it helps us to make wise decisions and stay on track with our goals.

Deductive reasoning is a skill that can be learned and improved with practice. So, if you want to be a better learner, start practicing your deductive reasoning skills today!

b. Inductive Reasoning

Inductive reasoning is a type of reasoning that uses specific examples to support a general conclusion. This type of reasoning is often used in scientific investigations where scientists will observe specific examples to form a hypothesis about how the world works.

Inductive reasoning is based on the principle that the truth of a general statement can be *inferred* from the truth of several specific cases. For example, if I see several cats scratching furniture, I might infer that all cats scratch furniture. Inductive reasoning is often used to create generalizations from observations.

One advantage of inductive reasoning is that it can lead to new discoveries. By observing specific examples and making generalizations based on those observations, scientists can uncover new facts about the world that they would not have otherwise known.

Another advantage of inductive reasoning is that it can help us make better decisions. By understanding the general principles that underlie specific examples, we can make better choices based on our knowledge and experience. For example, if we know that most cases of a particular disease are fatal, we can make a more informed decision about whether to seek medical attention if we think we may be infected.

While deductive reasoning is based on a set of specific rules, inductive reasoning is based on general observations and principles. Therefore, inductive reasoning is sometimes called "the scientific method." Scientists use inductive reasoning to formulate hypotheses, which they then test through experimentation.

WHY ARE THE TWO TYPES OF REASONING IMPORTANT IN LEARNING?

Inductive reasoning is used to develop a generalization from specific instances. This type of reasoning is often used in learning, as it allows us to form generalizations about a topic based on the information we have gained so far. Inductive reasoning can be helpful in allowing us to see patterns and relationships between different pieces of information. This can then allow us to build a more complete "Big Picture" understanding of the topic.

Inductive reasoning can also help us extrapolate to make predictions about future events. For example, if we know that a particular animal tends to hibernate during the winter, we can use inductive reasoning to predict that other animals of the same species will likely hibernate as well. Inductive reasoning can also help us to understand complex concepts by breaking them down into smaller pieces. By understanding these smaller pieces, we can begin to see the whole picture and understand how the different parts intersect and connect.

While inductive reasoning is often very helpful, it is important to remember that it is not always accurate. Just because something has happened in the past does not mean that it will happen in the future. Additionally, inductive reasoning can sometimes lead to false conclusions if the data is not properly analyzed.

Conversely, deductive reasoning is used to develop a specific instance from a generalization and therefore is often used in problem-solving. It allows us to identify specific steps that we can take to solve a problem. Deductive reasoning can also help us to see the limitations of a generalization. For example, if we know that all goldfish can swim, we can use deductive reasoning to identify a specific goldfish that cannot swim.

Deductive reasoning can also help us to understand complex concepts by breaking them down into smaller pieces. By understanding the smaller pieces, we are better able to see the big picture and understand the concept as a whole. Deductive reasoning is often used in mathematics and science, where complex concepts can be broken down into smaller steps that can be easily understood.

While inductive reasoning is often less accurate than deductive reasoning, it can be more helpful in everyday life. Inductive reasoning allows us to see the world around us in a more general way, which can help us to make better decisions. Additionally, inductive reasoning can help us to find patterns in data, which can be helpful in solving problems.

3. THE TWO LEARNING ENVIRONMENTS

The term *learning environment* refers to the way someone learns or the environment in which they learn. There are many types of learning environments such as active vs. passive learning, or student- vs. content-centered, or even the physical setting in which teaching and learning occur, which we will touch on here. The two types of learning environments we will look at are formal vs. informal, and interpersonal vs intrapersonal.

a. Formal and Informal Environments

Formal learning environments take place in a classroom or other educational setting and are generally structured, with a set curriculum that students must follow. The teachers in these environments typically have a lot of control over what and how the students learn. This type of learning is good for people who thrive on organization and discipline.

In contrast, informal learning environments occur outside of a classroom or educational setting and are more flexible; this type of learning environment allows students to learn based on their own interests and needs. Informal learning environments are often more creative and allow for more collaboration among students.

Ultimately, it is important to understand which learning environment is best for you. Some people thrive in a formal learning environment while others may prefer the more relaxed atmosphere of an informal learning environment. Once you understand your favored environment, it will be easier for you to pursue a better life.

The other classification is based on the actual nature of learning as an individual learner or as a social learner. There are two types of learning environments based in this classification: intrapersonal and interpersonal.

b. Intrapersonal and Interpersonal Environments

Intrapersonal learning takes place within the individual, while interpersonal learning takes place between people. Each environment has its own benefits and drawbacks when it comes to learning.

Intrapersonal learning is often associated with solitary activities, such as reading, writing, or reflecting on one's own thoughts. This can be beneficial because it allows learners to learn at their own pace and better focus on their needs. Intrapersonal learning can also help individuals understand their own strengths and weaknesses, which can be useful when it comes to making decisions or setting goals.

Drawbacks to intrapersonal learning are that learners may feel socially isolated, or they may get lost in their own thoughts. They also do not have the opportunity to mentor or be mentored by others who are below or above them with a skill.

By contrast, interpersonal learning is often associated with social activities, such as discussing ideas with others, working in collaborative teams, or giving presentations. This environment can be beneficial because it provides opportunities for you to share ideas and learn from each other. Interpersonal learning can also help you build relationships and develop communication skills.

One drawback to interpersonal learning is that it can be difficult to reach consensus or make decisions when working in a group. Another is that some people have more outgoing and assertive personalities than others and may dominate the project.

In the end, both intrapersonal and interpersonal learning environments have benefits and drawbacks. As you pursue a better life, consider which environment will work best for you, depending on your needs and goals.

CHAPTER 4

Learning from the Experts

With the advancement of technology, you can learn anything anywhere, anytime. Once you have chosen what you want to learn, the next question is, who will be your teacher? This is a very important question because the source of your knowledge will determine your destiny in life.

Nowadays, the Internet is becoming a more and more popular choice as the first source of any information that you want to know. You simply type any question into the search bar of any web browser, and you will see a lot of different answers from many sources.

Furthermore, social media is also getting more and more popular every single day. It is quickly becoming the number one source of information for most of the population. That's all well and good, but the downside to this is that you cannot be one hundred percent sure your source is reliable. So, be careful when you go online to search for answers to your questions. You might end up getting fake news.

Personally, I prefer to learn from experts rather than the Internet or social media.

But how do you know that the knowledge you want to learn comes from a real expert?

First you must investigate the background of the author and the veracity of the subject he or she is trying to impart to you. In other words, check and double check if the information is a proven fact or simply an opinion.

Check and double check their reputation, too. You can do this by typing their name + the word "reviews" and see what you find. True experts share knowledge based on their actual experiences in life.

SUBJECTIVE AND OBJECTIVE KNOWLEDGE

There are two categories of knowledge: subjective knowledge and objective knowledge.

Subjective knowledge is what we believe to be true, while objective knowledge is what is proven to be true. Subjective knowledge can be based on personal experiences, while objective knowledge is based on research or facts.

Subjective knowledge is one person's point of view and can be called personal knowledge. It is based on that person's individual experiences and opinions. Subjective knowledge can be open to interpretation.

Objective knowledge, on the other hand, can be called empirical knowledge. It is based on evidence that can be independently observed, replicated, and measured. Objective knowledge is less subject to interpretation than subjective knowledge.

It is important to be aware of the difference between subjective and objective knowledge, so you can better understand both yourself and others. But which type of knowledge is more important?

Some people might say that objective knowledge is more important because it is based on facts, and it can help us understand the world around us and make better decisions. Others might say that subjective knowledge is more important because it allows for different interpretations and individual beliefs, and it can help us understand people and their experiences.

Both types of knowledge have value. They should be used together to create a well-rounded understanding of the world. Objective knowledge is essential for comprehending the world around us and making better decisions. Subjective knowledge doesn't *allow* for different perspectives.

Because we as humans are emotional beings with consciences and freewill, we have subjective knowledge. Or more accurately, without our own complex perceptions of reality, we would be robots and thus would not have subjective knowledge. This brings us to our next concept: how we filter our knowledge.

SUBJECTIVE REALITY AND OBJECTIVE REALITY

There are two kinds of reality: subjective reality and objective reality.

In subjective reality, each person experiences life through their own unique filters, based on their individual beliefs, values, and life experiences. As a result, what one person sees as reality may be very different from what another person sees.

Objective reality, on the other hand, is the reality that exists independent of our individual perceptions. It is the reality that exists "out there" in the world regardless of what we think or believe.

Both subjective reality and objective reality are important, and each has its own unique value. However, to create the best life possible, it is important to learn how to navigate both realities effectively.

To navigate subjective reality, it is important to be aware of our own filters or lenses and to understand how they can distort our view of reality. It is also important to be authentic and honest with ourselves, and to stay true to our own values and beliefs.

HOW CAN I BECOME A TRUE EXPERT?

So how do you become a true expert? You start by learning from those who have gone before you. There are many ways to learn from the experts, but one of the best is to find a mentor. A mentor can guide you and teach you the ropes and can help you avoid common mistakes.

Another great way to learn is to read books written by experts. Not only will you learn the basics, but you'll also gain a deeper understanding of the topic.

Finally, don't be afraid to ask questions. Most experts are happy to share their knowledge, and you'll learn a lot by asking questions and engaging in discussion. By following these tips, you'll be on your way to becoming a true expert yourself.

Finding mentors or teachers who can help guide and teach you the ropes is just the first step. The next step is to make sure that you follow their advice and learn from your own experiences, then step into service by helping others. Only then will you truly be able to call yourself an expert.

Remember, being an expert is not about having all the answers or being a perfect human being but rather about knowing where to find the answers.

And finally, as you share your knowledge with others to help them grow and learn, you also enhance your own mastery, confidence, and happiness.

WHY IS IT IMPORTANT TO LEARN FROM EXPERTS?

For many reasons...

One: Experts have a wealth of knowledge and experience that they can share with you. They can teach you new things, show you how to do things better, help you avoid mistakes and learn from those you have already made.

Two: Another reason it is important to learn from the experts is that they can help you develop your own skills and talents. Experts know what it takes to be successful, and they can guide you on the path to achieving your goals.

And lastly, learning from experts can help you stay up to date with the latest trends and developments in your field. They can keep you informed about new techniques and technologies so you can further improve your work.

So, if you want to hone your skills, achieve your goals, and stay ahead of the curve, then learning from the experts is a great place to start.

WHO ARE SOME OF THE WORLD'S EXPERTS IN THE SELF-HELP INDUSTRY?

The experts in the self-help industry are those who have found success in helping others achieve success. They have a wealth of knowledge and experience to share and are passionate about helping others improve their lives. There are many experts in this field, but some of the most well-known include:

1. Tony Robbins
2. Oprah Winfrey
3. Wayne Dyer
4. Bob Proctor
5. Brian Tracy
6. Stephen R. Covey
7. Og Mandino
8. Napoleon Hill
9. Jim Rohn
10. Dale Carnegie

11. Zig Ziglar
12. Norman Vincent Peale
13. Les Brown
14. Jack Canfield
15. Bradley Sugars
16. Ken Blanchard
17. John Maxwell
18. Spencer Johnson
19. Thomas J. Stanley
20. Michael Gerber
21. Brendan Burchard
22. Tim Ferris
23. Robert B. Cialdini
24. Deepak Chopra
25. Eckhart Tolle
26. John Gray
27. David Schwartz
28. Richard Carlson
29. Paolo Coelho
30. James Clear

Let's get to know each of these experts for your reference.

1. Tony Robbins

Tony Robbins is one of the most well-known and respected self-help experts in the world. He has helped millions of people achieve their goals and improve their lives. Robbins is a highly sought-after speaker and has appeared on countless TV shows and podcasts. Robbins is the author of several best-selling books, including *Unlimited Power* and *Awaken the Giant Within*.

He is also the creator of the Robbins Learning Institute, which provides personal development training to people from all over the world. Robbins is known for his high-energy speeches and his ability to inspire people to change their lives for the better. He has helped people overcome addiction, deal with grief and loss, and set and achieve meaningful goals.

If you're looking for help in accomplishing your personal goals, Tony Robbins is one of the best self-help experts out there. He has a wealth of knowledge and experience to share, and his teachings can help you find lasting success.

2. Oprah Winfrey

Oprah Winfrey is one of the most influential women in the world and has been dubbed the Queen of All Media. She is a self-help expert who has hosted her own talk show, been a magazine publisher and CEO, and is now a television network owner and producer.

Oprah is known for her no-holds-barred interviews and her personal stories of overcoming adversity. Her advice is always heartfelt and based on her own experiences. She has helped millions of people improve their lives by teaching them how to be their own best friend and advocate.

3. Wayne Dyer

Wayne Dyer was one of the most well-known self-help experts in the world. He was the author of numerous books on the topic, including *Manifesting Change,* and *Change Your Thoughts, Change Your Life.* Dyer was a recognized expert on the topic of positive thinking and has helped millions of people learn to change their lives for the better.

Personally, Wayne Dyer is one of my favorite self-help experts. His books changed the way I think. I used his teachings as guideposts in my journey to pursue a better life. Literally, Wayne Dyer's teachings changed my life.

Dyer's philosophy was based on the idea that each of us has the power to create our own reality. He taught that by changing our thoughts, we can change our lives for the better. Dyer believed that we are all capable of creating our own happiness and success, and that by changing our thoughts and attitude, we can manifest positive change in our lives.

Dyer's teachings have helped millions of people around the world learn how to create positive change in their lives. He was a trusted source of advice and wisdom for people who are looking to improve their lives. If you are looking to make a positive change in your life, Wayne Dyer's writings will be a great place to start. I know I'm a bit biased with my recommendation, but if you follow the suggestions in his books, most likely, your life is also going to change for the better.

4. Bob Proctor

Bob Proctor was a self-help expert and the author of the book *You Were Born Rich*, where he discussed the eleven principles of success.

The first principle is having a definite purpose. You need to know what you want to achieve. The second principle is learning to think in terms of abundance, not scarcity. You need to focus on the positives and believe that you can have what you want in life.

The third principle is knowing your true power. You need to understand your own strengths and weaknesses to use them to your advantage. The fourth principle is taking massive action. You need to be willing to do whatever it takes to achieve your goals. The fifth is maintaining life balance. You can't focus on one area at the expense of the others.

The sixth principle is becoming a master of your emotions so you can use them to your advantage. The seventh principle is developing a healthy attitude toward money. You need to understand that money is simply a tool and not something to be feared. The eight is cultivating a winning mindset. You need to believe that you can achieve anything you set your mind to.

The ninth principle is surrounding yourself with likeminded people. You need to associate with people who will help you achieve your goals. The tenth is setting and achieving goals on a regular basis. You need to establish a routine and stick to it. The eleventh principle is using the power of positive thought. You need to think positively and focus on the things you want in life.

5. Brian Tracy

Brian Tracy is a motivational public speaker and self-development author. He has written over eighty books that have been translated into dozens of languages.

One of his popular books, *Eat That Frog!*, teaches people how to get more done in less time. He is also the president of a company that helps people achieve their personal and professional goals. If you're looking to get more done in less time, Brian Tracy is the expert to follow.

6. Stephen R. Covey

If you are looking for guidance and want to improve your life, then a self-help expert may be right for you like Stephen R. Covey. Covey is the author of *The 7 Habits of Highly Effective People*, which has sold more than 25 million copies. His book *The 8th Habit: From Effectiveness to Greatness* focuses on helping people find their passion in life and achieve great things.

Covey's books are packed with useful information and advice, and his approach is both down-to-earth and motivating. If you're ready to take your life to the next level, start with the two books I just mentioned. You won't regret it!

7. Og Mandino

Og Mandino was an expert in sales and motivation. He was also the author of *The Greatest Salesman in the World*. In this book, Mandino shares the wisdom he gained from his experiences as a salesman.

One of the best things about *The Greatest Salesman in the World* is that it is full of stories. These stories help to illustrate Mandino's points and make them easier to understand. In addition, they are just plain interesting to read.

One story that Mandino tells is about a man who was trying to sell a horse. He was having a lot of trouble finding a buyer, so he decided to go to a man who was known as the best horse trader in the area. When he got to the man's house, he found that the man was sick in bed.

The man told the salesman that he couldn't buy the horse, but he offered to teach the salesman how to trade horses. The salesman agreed, and the man taught him everything he knew. After just a few months, the salesman was able to trade horses like a pro and make a good living doing it.

Learning from the experts can be a great way to improve your skills in any area. If you want to learn how to trade horses like a pro, find someone who is good at it and ask them to teach you. You'll be surprised at how much you can learn in a short amount of time.

8. Napoleon Hill

Napoleon Hill was an expert on success. His classic 1937 bestseller *Think and Grow Rich* is about the thirteen steps to riches and has been read by millions of people. Hill interviewed over five hundred self-made millionaires to find out what made them successful.

One key to success, according to Hill, is having a definite chief aim in life. What is your chief aim? What are you working toward? Define your goals and put a plan in place to achieve them.

Another key to success is developing a mastermind group. A mastermind group is a group of people who come together to help each other achieve their goals by creatively brainstorming. The group should have a variety of skills and knowledge so that everyone can benefit.

Finally, Hill tells us to be persistent and don't give up. Success doesn't happen overnight; it takes time and effort. But if you keep working at it, you will eventually achieve your goals.

9. Jim Rohn

Jim Rohn was a personal development expert and one of the most influential speakers of his time. He was known for his philosophy that we are the sum of the people we've met and the books we've read.

Rohn was born in Yakima, Washington, in 1933. He started his career as a stockbroker but later became interested in personal development. He began to lecture in the early 1960s and quickly gained a following. Rohn's philosophy was that we should work to become the best versions of ourselves. We should surround ourselves with positive people and read positive books. We should also take action to improve our lives.

Rohn's teachings have been published in dozens of books, and he has been featured on television and radio programs around the world. He passed away in 2009.

10. Dale Carnegie

Dale Carnegie was a writer and lecturer on self-improvement. He wrote the book *How to Win Friends and Influence People,* which became an instant bestseller and is still popular today. Carnegie's philosophy was that most people want to be liked and feel important. He taught how to make others feel important through simple techniques like paying attention, being interested in them, and listening attentively.

Carnegie also taught how to handle difficult people and situations. His philosophy was that most people are reasonable if you treat them with respect. He gave useful tips on how to get along with others, including how to give compliments, make requests, and share your ideas. Dale Carnegie's advice is still relevant today, and his teachings can help you become a more likeable and successful person no matter what line of work you are in and what your socio-economic status, race, or creed.

11. *Zig Ziglar*

One of the most popular self-help experts of all time was Zig Ziglar. He wrote and spoke extensively on the topics of personal development, motivation, and success. He was known for his upbeat, positive attitude and his ability to motivate people to achieve their goals. Ziglar's philosophy was that everyone has the ability to be successful if they set their mind to it.

He taught that success is largely a matter of attitude, and that if you want something badly enough, you can find a way to get it. He also stressed the importance of taking action and making things happen in your life.

Zig Ziglar's advice was simple, but it was based on years of experience and research. He helped millions of people achieve their dreams, and his teachings continue to inspire people around the world.

12. *Norman Vincent Peale*

There is no doubt that Norman Vincent Peale was a pioneer in the self-help movement. He wrote *The Power of Positive Thinking*, one of the first books to popularize the power of positive thinking as a way to improve one's life.

Peale's philosophy is simple but powerful: if you focus on the good in life and think positively, you can achieve anything you want. His book has sold millions of copies and has been translated into dozens of languages.

Despite some criticism that his teachings are too simplistic or unrealistic, Peale's work has helped millions of people around the world achieve their goals and live happier lives. He was a true pioneer in the self-help movement and his legacy will continue to inspire people for years to come. I thought his book is as relevant today as it was before.

13. Les Brown

Best-selling author, motivational speaker, radio host, and entrepreneur, Les Brown is one of the world's most popular self-help experts. Brown's advice is based on the philosophy that we are capable of achieving anything we want if we set our minds to it. Brown has spent his life teaching people how to recognize and overcome the obstacles that stand in the way of their success. He urges his listeners and readers to take control of their lives and never give up on their dreams.

Brown's books, speeches, and seminars have helped millions of people around the world achieve their goals and improve their lives. He is a living example of the power of self-belief and determination, and his messages are more relevant than ever in today's fast-paced, constantly changing world.

14. Jack Canfield

Jack Canfield is a self-help author who has written best-selling books such as *The Success Principles.* He is also the co-creator of the wildly popular *Chicken Soup for the Soul* series.

Canfield's work is based on the idea that success is attainable for everyone. He teaches that by setting goals and taking action, anyone can achieve their dreams.

Canfield's books are full of inspiration and motivational advice. They offer tips and techniques for overcoming obstacles and achieving success. Canfield's teachings have helped millions of people around the world to live happier, more successful lives. His work is evidence that self-help can be life changing.

15. Bradley Sugars

For me, there is no one more qualified to talk about self-help than Bradley Sugars. A multimillionaire entrepreneur, Sugars knows what it takes to achieve success. In his book, *The Wealth Coach,* he lays out a simple formula for getting ahead in life.

But Sugars' advice isn't just for the wealthy. His principles are applicable to anyone who is willing to put in the hard work. Whether you're just starting out or you're already successful, *The Wealth Coach* can help you take your business or career to the next level.

Sugars is a believer in using failure as a learning experience. In fact, he says that if you're not failing, you're not trying hard enough. If you're stuck in a rut, *The Wealth Coach* can help you break out of it and achieve your goals.

On a personal note, I had the opportunity to be trained, coached, and mentored by Bradley Sugars throughout my business venture as the master franchisee of Action International, now ActionCOACH, for the entire country of the Philippines.

16. Ken Blanchard

Ken Blanchard is a well-known self-help expert. He is the co-author of the best-selling book *The One Minute Manager*. In this book, Blanchard teaches managers how to become more effective leaders by using one-minute goals and one-minute coaching sessions.

Blanchard is also the author of several other bestselling books, including *Leading at a Higher Level* and *Raving Fans*. He is a popular keynote speaker and has been featured on numerous television and radio programs.

What makes Blanchard such a successful self-help expert is his ability to make complex topics easy to understand. He has a gift for taking complicated theories and breaking them down into simple steps that anyone can follow. Blanchard also has a lot of experience in the business world, which gives him a unique perspective that resonates with his audiences.

17. John Maxwell

John Maxwell is one of the most popular self-help experts in the world. He is a *New York Times* best-selling author, and his books have sold more than 25 million copies. Maxwell is a pastor, speaker, and coach who has helped people from all walks of life achieve their goals and improve their lives. Maxwell's teachings are based on the principle that success is a result of growth and development. He believes that everyone has the potential to be successful, and he helps people unlock that potential by teaching them how to think and act like successful people.

Maxwell's philosophy is that success is not about what you have or what you do, it's about who you are. He teaches people how to develop the qualities that are essential for success, such as discipline, integrity, humility, and courage.

18. Spencer Johnson

Spencer Johnson was a self-help expert, co-author of *Who Moved My Cheese?* and of *The One-Minute Manager*. Johnson was a best-selling author who wrote more than twenty books on various topics such as self-help, business, health, and leadership. He was also a speaker and consultant who worked with organizations such as IBM, General Electric, and Microsoft.

Johnson's books are based on the premise that success can be achieved by taking a more simplified and straightforward approach to life. He believed that success is attainable by anyone who is willing to put in the effort, and that the key to success is to focus on the basics and keep things simple. His books provide readers with practical advice and easy-to-follow tips that can be applied to everyday life.

Johnson was a popular speaker and has been quoted as saying, "People often fail because they try to do too much. When you learn to do less, you can succeed." He was a firm believer in the philosophy of less is more, and his books provide readers with actionable advice that can be easily implemented into everyday life.

19. Thomas J. Stanley and William D. Danko

In their book *The Millionaire Next Door*, Thomas Stanley and William D. Danko outlined the seven common traits of America's wealthiest citizens. The book has become a self-help classic, and the authors have been quoted and interviewed by numerous media outlets. Stanley and Danko's research found that most millionaires don't live in fancy neighborhoods or drive expensive cars. They're the people next door who have worked hard, saved diligently, and invested wisely.

So, what can the rest of us learn from America's millionaires? Here are three of the most important lessons:

1. Don't be afraid to save money. Saving money is key to building wealth. Millionaires are typically good at living below their means and spending less than they earn. By creating a budget and sticking to it, you can do it, too!

2. Invest your money wisely. Millionaires invest a significant portion of their income in stocks, bonds, and real estate. By doing the same, you can grow your wealth steadily, in any market.

3. Be patient. Building wealth takes time. Don't get discouraged if you don't see results immediately. Stay the course, and you'll be on your way to financial success!

20. Michael Gerber

A former small business owner, Gerber is now a best-selling author and speaker on the topics of entrepreneurship and self-reliance. His books, including *The E-Myth Revisited* and *The E-Myth Manager,* have been translated into over thirty languages and have sold more than 5 million copies worldwide.

Gerber's teachings focus on the idea that everyone can be an entrepreneur regardless of their background or experience. Through his books, seminars, and online courses, Gerber has helped millions of people learn how to start and grow their own businesses. I can comfortably say that I am one of the millions of people that Michael Gerber had helped through his books and courses.

If you're looking for tips on how to be successful in life, Michael Gerber is one self-help expert you don't want to miss.

21. Brendan Burchard

Brendan Burchard is the founder and CEO of the High Performance Academy, a company that teaches people how to live an extraordinary life. He is the author of the best-selling book *The Millionaire Messenger,* and he has also written several other books including *The Charge, The Motivation Manifesto,* and *High Performance Habits.* He is a highly sought-after public speaker, and he has spoken at events all over the world.

Burchard's work is based on the idea that everyone has the potential to create an extraordinary life if they have the right tools and mindset. He teaches people how to set and achieve big goals, increase their productivity, improve their communication skills, and develop positive habits that will help them achieve success.

Burchard is a powerful example of what's possible when you commit to living an extraordinary life. He has overcome many challenges in his life and now uses his experiences to help others.

22. Tim Ferriss

Tim Ferriss is a life hacker and self-help expert. He is the author of the best-selling book *The 4-Hour Workweek.* Ferriss teaches how to "hack" your life to get more done in less time. He is a self-proclaimed "minimum viable everything" advocate, meaning that he enjoys testing out a variety of different tactics and strategies in order to find what works best for him.

Ferriss is also a proponent of the Slow-Carb Diet, which advocates eating mostly unprocessed foods and avoiding white carbohydrates. He has lost over sixty pounds as a result and claims that it has improved his overall health and energy levels.

While Ferriss' approach to self-help may be unconventional, it seems to be working well for him. He has inspired others to follow his lead and has helped many people achieve greater work-life balance and improved health.

23. *Robert B. Cialdini*

Robert B. Cialdini is a self-help expert and author of the book *Influence: The Psychology of Persuasion*. In it, Cialdini discusses the six principles of persuasion that can be used to influence people's behavior.

Cialdini's principles are based on decades of research into the psychology of persuasion.

The first principle is reciprocity. This principle states that people feel obligated to return a favor. If someone does something nice for you, you'll likely feel obligated to do something nice for them in return, which is why companies often send out free samples or offer discounts to customers. They want to create a sense of reciprocity so that the customer will be more likely to buy from them in the future.

The second principle is commitment and consistency. This states that people tend to behave in ways that are consistent with their earlier commitments. For example, if you make a commitment to go to the gym, you're more likely to follow through with that commitment if you've already paid for a membership or purchased some equipment.

The third principle is social proof. This states that people are influenced by the actions of others. For example, if you're not sure whether or not to buy a product, you might look at what other people are doing—if they're buying the product, you're more likely to buy it too.

The fourth principle is authority. This points out that people are more likely to comply with requests made by someone who is in a position of authority. For example, if your boss asks you to stay late at work, you're more likely to do it than if a coworker asks you the same thing.

The fifth principle is scarcity. This principle states that people perceive things that are in short supply as being more valuable. For example, if you know that there are only a few tickets left for a concert, you'll be more likely to want to buy one.

The sixth and final principle is liking. This principle states that people are more likely to comply with requests made by people they like. For instance, if you're getting a haircut, you're more likely to go with the hairstylist you like than the one you don't.

24. Deepak Chopra

Deepak Chopra is one of the most well-known self-help experts in the world. He is the author of more than fifty books on mind-body healing, spirituality, and personal growth. Chopra has been a medical doctor for more than twenty-five years, and he is also a professor of medicine at the University of California, San Diego.

Chopra's approach to self-help is based on the belief that we all have the potential to heal ourselves and to create lives of meaning and purpose. His books offer readers practical advice on how to overcome obstacles and create positive change in their lives.

Chopra's work has been praised by many experts in the fields of self-help and spirituality. His books are widely read and have been translated into more than thirty-five languages. He has also been honored with numerous awards, including the prestigious Martin Luther King Jr. Peace Award.

25. Eckhart Tolle

There is no question that Eckhart Tolle is a self-help expert. He has written several books on the subject, and his teachings have helped millions of people around the world.

What makes Tolle so unique is that he doesn't just focus on the positive aspects of life. He also talks about the negative aspects, and how to deal with them.

Tolle's approach to self-help is very holistic. He believes that the key to happiness and success is to be in tune with yourself and your surroundings. He teaches that it's important to be present in the moment and to live your life authentically.

Tolle's teachings are based on his own personal experiences. He has been through a lot in his life, and he has learned a lot from his experiences. This makes his teachings more credible, and it makes them easier to understand and apply.

26. John Gray

John Gray is a self-help expert known for his best-selling book *Men are from Mars, Women are from Venus*. Gray is a relationship coach who helps couples understand each other better. He has also written other books such as *Beyond Mars and Venus* and *How to Get What You Want and Want What You Have*. Gray is a popular speaker and has made many appearances on television and radio.

Gray's advice is based on his belief that men and women are from different "planets" and that they have different needs and communication styles.

He believes that men need to take charge and be the breadwinner, while women need to be nurtured and appreciated. Gray's advice can be helpful for couples who are struggling to understand each other. However, his advice should not be taken too seriously.

It is important to remember that every relationship is different, and what works for one couple may not work for another. Gray's advice should be used as a conversational starting point, not as the final word on relationships.

27. David Schwartz

David Schwartz was one of the world's leading self-help experts. He wrote many books, including *The Magic of Thinking Big* and *The Power of Intention*. David's work was based on the principle that success is achievable by anyone who sets their mind to it. He has helped millions of people around the world achieve their goals and live happier, more fulfilling lives.

If you're looking for advice on how to achieve success and happiness, David Schwartz is definitely someone worth listening to. His books are packed with helpful tips and strategies that will help you get the most out of life.

28. Richard Carlson

Richard Carlson was an American self-help author who wrote several best-selling books on the topic of personal development. He is best known for his book *Don't Sweat the Small Stuff... and It's All Small Stuff*, which has sold over 20 million copies.

Carlson began his writing career in the early 1990s after being inspired by a self-help book he read while recovering from a car accident. He penned his first book, *You Can Do It! The Mini*

Guide to Accomplishing Anything, in just two weeks and followed up with *Don't Sweat the Small Stuff... and It's All Small Stuff* a year later.

Carlson's books focus on developing a positive outlook and reducing stress levels. He advocates for living in the present and taking things one step at a time. Carlson passed away in 2006 at the age of fifty-three, but his legacy lives on through his many best-selling books.

If you're looking for some tips on how to live a happier and less stressful life, then Richard Carlson is your man. His books are full of helpful advice on how to achieve inner peace and live in the present moment. If you're feeling overwhelmed by life's challenges, then his books could be just what you need to get back on track.

29. Paolo Coelho

Paolo Coelho is one of the most renowned self-help experts in the world. He is the author of many internationally best-selling books, including *The Alchemist, The Pilgrimage,* and *The Manual of the Warrior of Light.* Coelho's books offer spiritual guidance and advice on how to live a meaningful and fulfilling life.

Coelho's approach to self-help is based on the idea that we all have the power to create our own destiny. He believes that by following our dreams and passions, we can achieve happiness and fulfillment.

Coelho's books are full of inspirational quotes and messages that encourage readers to pursue their dreams and live life to the fullest.

If you're looking for some inspiration and guidance on how to live a happier and more gratifying life, then I recommend checking out some of Paolo Coelho's books. His writing is truly inspiring, and his advice is worth hearing.

30. *James Clear*

James Clear is a self-help expert who teaches people how to improve their productivity, health, and happiness. He has written a book—*Atomic Habits*—and has a popular blog where he shares his tips for living a better life.

Clear's philosophy is based on the idea that small changes can make a big difference in your life. He believes that if you can make small, consistent changes to your habits, you can achieve big results.

Clear's approach to self-help is simple and easy to follow, and his writing is engaging and motivating. He provides clear instructions for making changes in your life, and he offers helpful tips and advice for staying on track.

If you're looking for help improving your productivity, health, or happiness, James Clear is a good place to start. His books and blog are packed with useful information.

These individuals have helped tens of millions of people around the world change their lives for the better, and they continue to share their wisdom and guidance with others.

If you're looking for help improving your life, then it's worth seeking out advice from one of the experts in the self-help industry. They can teach you how to set and achieve goals, overcome obstacles, and live a happier and more fulfilling life. By learning from the experts, you can increase your chances of achieving success in your own life.

CHAPTER 5

The Three Conditions for Learning

There are certain conditions you need to comply with before you can begin your journey into the amazing world of knowledge acquisition, and these conditions will assure you that you can get the most out of your learning.

The first condition to maximize your learning is to *open your mind*.

I know you've heard it before, but I'm going to say it again. Our mind is like a parachute; it only works when it's open. So that's what I'm going to ask you to do: Open your mind. I can almost hear you saying, I'm willing to open my mind but how? That's a valid question. As a matter of fact, most people don't really know how to open their mind. They don't understand what it means to open their mind. This is one of the many actions we know we should do but we never learn *how* to do it.

At this point I would like to share with you a very powerful technique on how to open your mind so that you can really maximize your learning potential.

You must decide to become a student of life.

You must make a conscious decision to be learning all the time.

In other words, stop acting like a know-it-all. Have you ever experienced this on the receiving end? It's no fun, right? You haven't even finished saying what you wanted to say, and the other person is already shutting down, thinking, "I know that already" and jumping in to try to "one up" you. Don't be that kind of person.

Being a student of life is a matter of attitude. Always consider the possibility that *you can learn something from anybody*. It doesn't matter what the person's level of education is or his or her status in life. What really matters is being open to the possibility of learning something new all the time. Consider every day and every moment an opportunity for a fresh, new learning experience, and you will be amazed at how your attitude will change.

To become a student of life, you also need to be honest with yourself. Don't just say, "I am an open-minded person." The conviction must come from within, from the core of your being.

The second condition to maximize your learning potential is to ***open your heart.***

Now what do I mean by that? Let me explain. Opening our mind may not be a difficult thing to do, but then you must ask yourself: How do I determine the genuineness of my actions? There are some theories in psychology that indicate the human heart has a mind of its own. In other words, if you believe what you are saying, you can feel the rightness of it in your heart, which determines whether or not you are just offering lip service. So, to maximize your learning, you need to open your heart, too.

Don't be too concerned if you don't feel your words in your heart. This simply portrays how our minds have been conditioned and programmed based on our senses. Opening your heart also means being compassionate. If you have had some painful experiences in life, even back in your childhood, you may have partially closed your heart, and deeper healing will be needed to repair that. For now, suffice it to say that our minds and hearts should be synchronized, meaning, what I say is what

I really mean and feel inside. Open your mind as you open your heart.

The third condition to maximize your learning potential is **to unlearn.**

Our most difficult obstacle in learning is not our lack of willingness and determination to learn, but rather our lack of willpower to unlearn our old ways of thinking in order to create space for the new ways of learning.

Most people live their lives trying to defend what they think they know rather than allowing themselves to learn new ways of doing things or new ways of learning.

It's not easy to unlearn. How can you unlearn what you have already lived for more than say, 30, 40, 50, or 60 years of your life? Why do we have to unlearn anyway? What's wrong with what we already knew? Well, sometimes we must re-evaluate what we have learned in life. Sometimes we must question our belief, our values, the principles that we try to follow in our life.

The only constant thing in the universe is change. Everything evolves and changes every day. Some of the things you have already learned may have changed. A new scientific discovery or new historical evidence could change the way you view something. You have to be open to rediscovering what you thought you already knew.

Our environment is ever evolving. In a few minutes, days, weeks, months, years, what we already knew about a technology or theory becomes obsolete again, and we need to learn again. For example, everyone once thought the Earth was the center of the solar system. Now we know the Sun is.

The cycle of learning continues, and it's very important to keep updated of what's happening around you. Read books and articles on the latest ideas and schools of thought on various matters that interest you. After all, we know that life is a continuous learning process. We never stop learning so enjoy your learning journey.

SECTION TWO

Setting S.M.A.R.T. GOALS

CHAPTER 6

What Is Your Dream in Life?

At seventeen years old, I realized that my calling, my vocation, my dream was to help others. But I did not know how to do it. So, I looked to my parents for guidance to show me how to pursue this dream. They taught me that to be successful in anything, first I needed to pursue a better life for myself and later for my own family. Then and only then would I be able to fulfill my calling to help others.

Unlike me, you may not have discovered your dream at an early age. Maybe you are still grappling with your dream or your passion. You need to find out what interests you and go for it, even if later your dream changes.

One of my coaches taught me that everything starts with a dream. All authors of all the success books I have read talk about a dream as the starting point of becoming successful in your own business, in your own career, and in your own life.

American poet Carl Sandburg said, "Nothing happens unless first a dream."

The first key to success in Dr. Napoleon Hill's classic success book *Think and Grow Rich* is to find out what is your definite major purpose in life. The theme of Rick Warren's book *The Purpose Driven Life* is to answer the question: What on Earth am I here for?

So, the first step is to find your dream. What is it that mainly dominates your thought process every day? What is it that keeps burning deep inside you, keeping you awake late at night, and wakes you up very early the following morning? The answer to this question is your calling, your purpose, your dream.

If you already know what your dream is, congratulations! Maybe you've had a dream for as long as you can remember, or maybe it's something that popped into your head recently. But what do you do with it now? How do you make it happen? It's time to start taking some steps to make it a reality.

First, you need to figure out what you actually need to do to make your dream happen. This may involve doing some research or talking to people who have already achieved your dream, in their own way. What steps did they take? What did they do to make their dream a reality?

This is exactly what my life mentor told me many years ago. He said you can shortcut your way to achieving what you want in life. The first thing you need to do, he said, is to find someone who already did it before you and ask him how he did it. Then follow that path.

CHAPTER 7

What Are SMART Goals?

The next step is to set a goal or goals that will eventually lead you to make your dream a reality. We all know what it feels like to set a goal. You have an image of what you want, and you put all your focus and energy into making it happen. The problem is many times we set goals that are impossible to achieve. We get so focused on the result that we don't take the time to plan out how we're going to get there.

The best way to make sure your goals are achievable is to set SMART Goals. SMART stands for: Specific, Measurable, Achievable, Relevant, and Time-Bound.

SMART Goals are:
Specific
Measurable
Achievable
Relevant
Time-Bound

By following these guidelines, you can be sure that your goals will be realistic and doable. When you set SMART Goals, you're more likely to achieve them. And make sure to have some fun along the way!

First, make sure your goal is specific and measurable. Don't just say, "I want to be thinner." Say, "I want to lose ten pounds by the end of the month." You need to have a way to track your progress, so you know if you've reached your goal or not. A goal is not achievable if you don't have a way to measure it.

Make sure your goal is relevant to your life and what you want to get done. Don't set a goal just for the sake of setting a goal. For example, don't set a goal to save money if you hate saving money. Finally, make sure your goal has a timeline attached to it. You need to have a date by which you want to achieve your goal.

I understand this task is not easy for some people. The SMART goal-setting formula is a common tool used to help individuals create effective goals. These five words help you set goals that are achievable and relevant to you. Specific goals are easier to measure and accomplish, while measurable goals give you a tangible way to track your progress.

Attainable goals challenge you but are still possible, while relevant goals are important to you and your life. Finally, time-bound goals give you a deadline to work toward, so you stay on track.

Here are some examples of SMART Goals:

Example 1: SMART Goal to Improving My Vocabulary

1. Specific: I will read more books this year than last year.
2. Measurable: I will read one book a month or more.
3. Achievable: I will select books that are within my reading level.
4. Relevant: Reading more will help me improve my vocabulary.
5. Time-Bound: I will complete my goal by December 31.

Example 2: SMART Goal to Meet My Business Objectives

1. Specific: I will boost my sales this year.
2. Measurable: I will increase my sales by 20% each month.

3. Achievable: I have the resources and ability to increase my sales by 20%.
4. Relevant: This goal will help me meet my overall business objectives.
5. Time-Bound: I will complete this goal by December 31.

Example 3: SMART Goal to Increase My Rainy-Day Fund

1. Specific: I will increase the rainy-day fund.
2. Measurable: I will save $500 per month to have an additional savings cushion of $6,000.
3. Achievable: I will consult with my financial advisor to create a plan that is realistically doable for me.
4. Relevant: I want to save for a rainy-day fund so that I am prepared for any unexpected expenses.
5. Time-Bound: I will complete this goal by the end of the year.

Setting goals is vital for achieving a dream but making sure they are SMART goals is just as important. Don't get carried away with unrealistic goals. And don't get overwhelmed or disheartened by not being able to measure your progress. Keep the prize in mind and track your steps to get there.

CHAPTER 8

Are You Aiming for Prosperity?

There are many different perspectives on prosperity, but most people believe that prosperity is something that can be achieved through hard work and determination. Some people believe that prosperity is a state of mind, while others believe that it is something that can be achieved through financial security. Prosperity is a state of being or an experience that is associated with having an abundance of money or possessions. Prosperity is a state of being prosperous, flourishing, or successful. It is often thought of as a state of happiness and well-being. Prosperity can bring feelings of happiness, comfort, and security.

It can also provide opportunities to travel, learn new things, and enjoy life's pleasures. However, when someone is too focused on material possessions, they can become spoiled and unappreciative of what they have. Additionally, excessive materialism can lead to greed, envy, and other destructive emotions.

No matter what your perspective on prosperity is, there are certain things that are required if you want to be and also feel prosperous. You need to understand what prosperity means to you and to develop a plan of action that will help you achieve your goals.

Stay positive, stay healthy, stay focused, and stay motivated, and you will be on your way to real prosperity.

HOW DO YOU ACHIEVE PROSPERITY IN LIFE?

There are many ways. For some people, it may mean having a lot of money, for others it may mean having a lot of tangible things, a big, beautiful house, and a great car, for some it means having a lot of free time, and for others it may mean having a lot of happiness and fulfilling relationships. No matter what your definition of prosperity is, there are certain things you can do to help you manifest it.

HERE ARE A FEW TIPS:

1. Be intentional.

If you want to be prosperous, you need to consciously focus on it. When you focus on what you want, you create a force field of energy that helps to manifest those things into your life.

2. Visualize what prosperity looks like for you.

When you visualize what prosperity looks like for you, it helps you to create a clear picture in your mind of what you want to achieve. The more detail and positive emotion you can put into your visualization, the better.

3. Believe that you can be prosperous.

One of the most important things you need to do to be prosperous is to believe you can be prosperous and that you deserve it. If you don't believe this, then you won't take the necessary actions to achieve it, or you will subconsciously sabotage your results.

4. Take action.

To be prosperous, you need to take action. This means setting goals and taking the necessary steps to achieve them. It also means being proactive and not waiting for things to happen.

5. Stay positive.

The key to achieving prosperity is to stay positive and focused on what you want, not on what you don't want. When you have a positive attitude, it helps to attract good things into your life.

6. Be patient.

Prosperity doesn't happen overnight. It takes time and patience. But if you stay focused and stay positive, you will eventually reach your goals.

7. Believe in yourself.

You are the key to your own prosperity. Believe in yourself and your ability to fulfill your goals. When you believe in yourself, you open yourself up to limitless possibilities.

8. Give thanks.

Be grateful for what you have in your life. When you pay attention to the good things, it attracts more good things into your life. Giving thanks is a powerful way to manifest prosperity into your life.

CHAPTER 9

To Go or Not to Go?

Once you have set some SMART Goals that will eventually lead you to fulfill your dream in life, it's now time to make some serious assessments as to where these goals can best be accomplished. I'm talking about actual moving here. You need to assess whether to stay where you currently are or to move to another location to achieve your goals.

If, after a thorough assessment of your goals, you decide you can get there from where you are, that's great. I wish you all the very best. If you decide you will need to move somewhere else, then create a concrete plan on how to make that happen.

In my own pursuit of a better life, I made one of the most difficult decisions of my life: to migrate to Australia with my family. The year was 1991, and I was scared to death. I mean, wouldn't you be?

> *Moving to a foreign country with no idea how everything was going to pan out was a terrifying decision.*

It's funny how your mind tricks on you. I heard this voice in my head called self-doubt: "Should I go or stay? Am I really going to leave everything behind?" Then I remembered a quote I read once: "The biggest risk is not to take risk at all." And so, after a thorough deliberation and discussion with the family, my wife and three little children, we made the most difficult family decision in our family life. We decided to go.

With heaps of doubt and apprehension but full of trust in the omnipotence and mercy of God, we left the Philippines in November 1991. As I'm writing this book, I look back and can only say, I am so grateful to the Almighty God that I made that decision to migrate to Australia. However, to say that we had a difficult start is a complete understatement.

When we first arrived, we shared a two-bedroom unit with six other members of my wife's family. For the first four months, I struggled to find a job. I sent probably more than one hundred applications for different job positions to different companies, big and small, but all I got was rejection.

I began to doubt my decision and thought I made the biggest mistake in my entire life. All kinds of questions popped out of my head, and I started to feel depressed. And I hate to admit it, but there were times when I felt worthless. My self-esteem went down the drain and I could no longer think of any reason why I should remain in Australia.

So, in March 1992, I decided to go back to the Philippines and promised myself not to set foot in this foreign land ever again. I told my wife and my children that I'd go first and prepare everything back home. Then they would follow later. I thought it was a good plan.

Although my wife was very hesitant, she agreed. So, they flew back to the Philippines a month later. By April 1992, we were all back in our home in Cebu, Philippines. We hadn't sold our house just in case we decided to come back. And we did.

Everything was back to how it was before we left the country six months earlier. I was back at my old job and the kids were preparing to go back to their old school. My wife decided not to go back to her work, so she could take care of the kids. I refurbished our house with a brand-new set of furniture and appliances.

After a month, the kids began showing some signs that they were not happy to go back to their old school. My wife and I had a very serious discussion about our situation, and then we had a family meeting. I asked the kids where they wanted to continue with their studies, and all of them shouted in unison, "Australia!" My wife looked at me. I looked at her, and we said, "OK, let's go back to Australia."

But this time, it was a different story altogether. I sold everything: the cars, the house, all the appliances, and the furniture we had just bought. This time, I told my family, "We'd better make it in Australia or else!" So, after everything was ready, we flew back to the land down under on our wedding anniversary, June 30, 1992. In the plane I thought, "Now that I've burned all my bridges, there's no turning back."

The decision had been made. I was thirty-five years old. My reality had changed. I was now living in a foreign country which would soon become the home of my family. So, for the next thirty years, I had to follow the plan I created in pursuing a better life for me and my family in Australia.

CHAPTER 10

Is Having a Dream Enough to Succeed?

"In order to succeed in life, you must have a dream!"

I must have heard motivational speakers shout these words from stage at least one hundred times, and I couldn't agree more. Yes, it is imperative to have a dream to succeed in life.

It naturally follows the line of thinking that advocates the power of the human mind. As Napoleon Hill put it so profoundly in his classic success book *Think and Grow Rich*: "Whatever the mind of man can conceive and believe it can achieve."

But, is that all it takes to succeed? Is having a dream enough to succeed in life? The answer is: No. Having a dream is not enough to succeed in life. It's only the beginning. Having a dream is the first step to success.

For the past thirty years, I have monitored the lives of twelve prominent people from different professions and in different stages in life. I tracked their status and net worth as individuals. And in summary, these are the results.

Out of the twelve people, four are already dead. Three left their original callings and pursued different professions, which unfortunately did not turn out well and made them miserable people. Two changed their genders and lived a miserable double life.

One became a billionaire quickly, then lost everything. One is in his seventies and still very actively pursuing his mission to help people through his ministry.

And one is Brian Tracy, and he's very much alive and very actively involved as the CEO of his own company, Brian Tracy International.

All the people I monitored had dreams. However, some of them did not continue pursuing their dreams. They lost focus, and they lost heart. Remember, having a dream is just the first step.

The second step is to continue working on it day in and day out until your dream comes true. The real challenge is that most people fail to squarely face the struggles along the way, and instead they give up. I can give you many real-life examples of people who are in this state of mind.

I am a music teacher, and in my music studio I teach piano, guitar, or singing lessons. Students are usually very excited to start their first lessons. After a month or so, some of them quit. After a few more months, more will quit.

On average, only 20 percent finish their first level of music learning. And this happens time and time again. Most people don't finish what they start.

After more than forty years of teaching music, I have seen this happen year after year. So, I asked myself, how can I help my students stay enrolled and stick to their decision of learning music?

I have tried a lot of strategies and still haven't found the answer. One time I decided to offer a free course hoping that they would stick to their lessons at least until they achieve some level of competency in their chosen musical instrument. And most of the attendees to this free course were already enrolled in my one-on-one music lessons in guitar and piano and singing. Reality happened again. Out of the twenty-seven original attendees, only two people finished the course. Eventually, all of them quit their individual lessons before they achieved any level of competency at all.

So, what is the secret to success? Why is it that some people succeed and some people don't. The answer is very simple: those who succeed continue what they started and persevered to the finish line.

Discipline your thoughts and control your mind to do only the activities that will help you achieve your goals and fulfill your dreams.

Our mind is the most powerful tool we have as human beings and it goes anywhere we want it to go. To become successful in life you need to keep on keeping on despite all the problems and challenges you encounter.

HERE ARE SIX STEPS THAT MIGHT HELP YOU:

1. *Make sure that your dream is bigger than your fear.*

You must keep your dream burning deep inside you every day and expand your comfort zone and stretch yourself to a point where your only option is to succeed.

2. *Decide to become a student of life.*

Decide to make continuous learning a part of your daily routine. For example, read a personal development book twenty minutes a day. I promise you, if you follow this advice, you will become a better person after one year or even less.

3. Surround yourself with positive and successful people.

Avoid associating yourself with negative people. Create a positive environment at home and at work to help you focus on your goals and on your dreams. This also means being selective about with whom you share your dream. Positive people will cheer you on and offer good advice. Don't give the naysayers any ammo to shoot down your dream!

4. Explore possibilities and opportunities and take some risks.

You'll never know what you can do unless you try. The worst thing that can happen is you will learn from your mistakes. But at least you took the chance. Did you know that the average millionaire will file for bankruptcy more than three times? They succeed because they keep taking chances, and they keep moving forward.

5. Test and measure different success strategies.

My business mentor, Bradley Sugars taught me how to try success strategies both in business and in my personal life. Don't hesitate to try some strategies that you can experiment on. After a given period, you will be able to determine which strategies work, and which didn't. The next move is to stop doing those that did not work and continue doing the ones that did work.

6. *Ask for help from an expert.*

Never be too proud to ask for some guidance from a life or business coach whose main goal is only to help you achieve what you set out to do in life.

These six steps will keep your focus on achieving your objectives. It's good to have a dream, but if you want to become successful in life, stick to the work you need to do with the right mindset and keep working at it to make your dream come true.

SECTION THREE

DETERMINATION
and Persistence

CHAPTER 11

Determination and Persistence

Determination is the commitment to achieving your goal no matter what stands in your way. It's the stubborn refusal to give up, even when the odds seem stacked against you. It's what allows you to pick yourself up after a failure and keep moving forward.

Persistence is the ability to keep going even when you're feeling tired or discouraged.

It's the quality that keeps you working toward your goal no matter how long it takes or how hard it gets.

If you are determined to achieve your goals, and you persist even when things get tough, then you will be more likely to succeed. When you have these qualities, you will be able to keep moving forward no matter what challenges you face.

So, if you are looking to improve your life, then determination and persistence are two qualities you should cultivate. These qualities are necessary to achieve success, both in life and in business.

In my experience, I have found that determination and persistence are essential qualities to have, if you want to achieve your goals. When I am determined to do something, I put in the effort to make it happen—no matter how challenging it may be. And when I am persistent, I don't give up on my goals, no matter how difficult they may be (or seem) to achieve.

These qualities have helped me to achieve success in both my personal and professional life.

The importance of both determination and persistence was highlighted for me when I started a new job here in Australia. I had been out of work for a while and was eager to find a new position. I applied for several jobs, but I didn't get any interviews. I was starting to get discouraged, but I didn't give up. I kept applying for jobs, and I kept networking.

Finally, I was offered a job that I really wanted. The lesson that I learned from this experience is that if you are determined and persistent, you will eventually find success. There are a lot of things we go through in life that try to knock us down. But it's important to remember that with determination and persistence, we can overcome anything.

So how do you apply determination and persistence in your life?

HERE ARE A FEW TIPS:

1. Set your goals high and be willing to work for them.

It's important to have a clear idea of what you want to achieve in life. Aim high and be willing to put in the work to make it happen. Don't be afraid to push yourself and shoot for the stars.

2. Stay positive and don't give up.

When things get tough, it's easy to give up or lose hope. But it's important to stay positive and keep moving forward. Remember, failure is a part of the process, and it's only through perseverance that you can achieve your goals.

3. Take action and don't wait for things to happen.

To achieve success, you must act and make things happen. You can't just sit around and wait for things to fall into your lap.

You must be proactive and put in the work necessary to reach your goals.

4. Persevere through the tough times.

There will be times when you face obstacles and setbacks. But it's important to keep moving forward and never give up. You must remember that the journey is often more important than the destination. And by persevering through the tough times, you'll eventually reach your goals.

CHAPTER 12

Work Smarter, Not Harder

There are many reasons why someone would want to work hard. One reason is that it's an important element in building a better life. When you work hard, you put yourself in a better position to achieve your goals. You also learn new skills and develop a work ethic.

Working hard also helps you stay focused and motivated. It can be easy to get sidetracked, but when you have a goal in mind, you are more likely to stay on track.

Another reason to work hard is because it's the right thing to do. When you work hard, you're doing your part to contribute to society and make the world a better place. You're also setting a good example for others.

Finally, working hard is rewarding in itself. You feel accomplished and proud of what you've done. When you achieve something through hard work, it feels great.

It will help you achieve your goals and feel good about yourself. And that's definitely worth it! You can learn new skills, make new connections, and gain experience that will help you reach your goals. So why not work hard?

WORKING SMARTER

Most people work hard because they believe this will help them achieve their goals. Hard work can be a powerful motivator, and it can also produce positive results. And, yes, in many cases, working hard is crucial to achieve success.

> *However, there are times when it's important to work smarter, not harder.*

There are a few reasons why working smarter can be even more effective than working hard. First, working smarter allows you to focus on your strengths. When you're trying to do too many things at once, you may not be able to do them as well as you'd like. By focusing on your strengths, you can accomplish your goals with better quality.

Second, working smarter allows you to take advantage of opportunities. If you're always working hard, you may not have time to take advantage of opportunities that come your way. However, if you're working smart, you can take advantage of these synchronicities and improve your business or career.

Finally, working smarter can help you avoid burnout. If you're always working hard, you may eventually reach a point where you're too tired to continue. This can lead to burnout, which can be harmful to your career or business. By working smart, you can avoid this problem and stay productive for longer.

In short, working smarter is often more effective than working hard. It allows you to focus on your strengths, take advantage of opportunities, and keep you energized. If you want to be successful, it's important to learn how to work smart.

WHAT DOES IT REALLY MEAN TO WORK SMARTER, NOT JUST HARDER?

To work smarter not harder means working on tasks that will have the most impact, delegating where possible, and optimizing your time and energy.

You can work smarter by setting aside time each week for planning and organizing and by developing productive habits. For example, try batching related tasks together to save time and energy. Instead of checking your email every five minutes, set aside specific times throughout the day to check it. This will prevent you from being interrupted every few minutes and allow you to focus on one task at a time.

Additionally, try to eliminate distractions so you can focus on your work. Turn off notifications on your phone and computer and put away any unnecessary objects in your work area.

If you're looking for more ways to work smarter, check out the following resources:

1. *The Productivity Project: Accomplish More by Managing Your Time, Attention, and Energy* by Chris Bailey

2. *The 4-Hour Workweek: Escape 9-5, Live Anywhere, and Join the New Rich* by Tim Ferriss

3. *Eat That Frog! 21 Great Ways to Stop Procrastinating and Get More Done in Less Time* by Brian Tracy

Are you looking for ways to be more productive and get more done in less time? If so, you're not alone. According to a study by the American Psychological Association, 43 percent of Americans feel overwhelmed by the amount of work they have to do.

There are plenty of resources available to help you increase your productivity both online and offline. Below are some of the tips I learned over the years and helped me achieve more in less time. Try these simple tips so you can make the most of your time and get more done.

HERE ARE SOME OF THEM:

1. Start by creating a to-do list and prioritizing the items.

2. Break down large tasks into smaller steps and make a plan for how you will achieve them.

3. Set deadlines for yourself and use a timer to help you stay on track.

4. Take short breaks to refresh your mind, stretch and move, and avoid distractions such as the Internet and social media.

5. Eliminate unnecessary tasks and delegate responsibilities where possible.

6. Streamline your workflow by creating templates and using shortcuts.

7. Be mindful of your energy levels and take time for self-care. Take time for yourself to relax and recharge so that you can be at your best when you're working.

ADVANTAGES OF WORKING SMARTER NOT HARDER

Working hard is great, but working smart is better. It's all about finding the right balance between putting in the effort and taking advantage of the tools and strategies at your disposal.

HERE ARE A FEW REASONS WHY WORKING SMARTER IS BETTER:

1. *You'll get more done.*

   When you're focused and organized, you can achieve more in less time.

2. *You'll be less stressed out.*

   Juggling multiple tasks can be overwhelming, but if you take advantage of helpful tools and strategies, you'll be more relaxed, peaceful, and also more productive.

3. *You'll have more time for yourself and whatever is important to you.*

   When you work smarter, you'll have more time to relax and enjoy your relationships, hobbies, and interests.

4. *You'll be more efficient.*

   By taking advantage of technology and other helpful tools, you can complete tasks quickly and efficiently.

5. *You'll be more successful.*

   Smart work habits will help you achieve your goals and reach your full potential.

CHAPTER 13

The Cycle of Success

The Cycle of Success consists of three stages:

1. *The Learning Stage*
2. *The Doing Stage*
3. *The Teaching Stage.*

Yes, successful people follow a cycle of learning, doing, and teaching. And if you are prepared to follow this cycle in your life, you, too can become more successful.

HOW CAN YOU BENEFIT FROM THE CYCLE OF SUCCESS?

You benefit from the Cycle of Success by passing on what you know, your wisdom as well as your knowledge, with the next generation or with someone who doesn't know as much. This sharing brings fulfillment on both sides.

The first step is learning. We are constantly discovering new things. Whether it is from a book, a teacher, or our own experiences, if we pay attention, we are always expanding our knowledge.

The second step is doing. Once we have learned what we need to know, we can put it into practice by doing what we have learned. This can be a challenging step, but it is also where the real learning takes place.

The third step is teaching. Once we have put what we have learned into practice by applying it, we can teach it to others. We do this by sharing our knowledge and experiences with others in a way that they can understand. This final step not only completes the Cycle of Success, but it also helps to spread the benefits to even more people.

This is a simple formula that has been followed by many successful people. You learn. You do. You teach. This process can be repeated, making you more successful with each cycle.

Prosperous people know the importance of learning new things throughout their lives. They also know the importance of taking action toward their goals. Finally, they understand the value of teaching others the things they have learned, helping them to achieve their own success.

Follow this simple formula, and you can achieve anything you set your mind to.

In my own life, I looked at the Cycle of Success and converted it into a formula. I tricked myself to become successful by following the formula of learning, doing, and teaching. This formula is very simple, but it is not easy.

Let me explain each step a little bit more.

1. THE LEARNING STAGE

Before you decide what you need to learn, you need to be very clear about the reason *why* you're going to learn it in the first place. For example, you only study medicine if you want to become a successful doctor. You only study law if you want to become a successful lawyer. In other words, you must decide what you need to study based on what career you want to pursue.

But even more importantly, tap into the why beneath your why. Why do you want to become a doctor or lawyer? The worst thing in life is to study something that you never really wanted to become successful at in the first place.

One of my clients revealed to me during our coaching session that he never really wanted to become a lawyer. It was his mother who wanted him to be a lawyer. He wanted to be a successful business owner in the telecommunications industry. When I was coaching him, he already had his first cell phone store. "Are you still working as a lawyer?" I asked him. "Not anymore," he told me. After a year of working there, he told his mother what he really wanted to do.

Therefore, it is very important to define your purpose and be very clear about it before you start learning.

After learning what you need to in your chosen field, you are then able to enhance your skills, build your confidence, and pursue your dream. So, learn as much as you can. Don't just rely on the general education you got from school. There are so many other sources of learning.

The Internet offers a vast network of resources where you can learn about anything. Explore audio and video materials that are readily accessible and convenient for you to use. There are so many books, magazines, and trade journals that will help you gain knowledge.

Just be sure the materials you are reading are written by someone who is already successful. Of course, when you have the opportunity, it is a must that you attend live seminars or workshops presented by people such as Brian Tracy, Bradley Sugars, Michael Gerber, or local business professionals in your area.

So now you've got the idea. The first stage in the Cycle of Success is to learn what you need to in your chosen field.

2. THE DOING STAGE

Learning is only the beginning of your journey to success. After you acquired enough of the specialized knowledge and education, perhaps even some certifications or credentials (although these are not always essential), you are now ready to implement what you have learned and do what you know. You might get a job in your field where you work for someone else doing what your qualifications allow you to do.

If you are in a job environment right now, remember two reasons why you are there: First, to learn more. Second, to build capital so that later you can apply your experience and knowledge into building your own business. If you are already working in and on your own business right now, congratulations! Keep up the good work. You are on the right track to success.

Don't get me wrong. I am not against having a job. As a matter of fact, I encourage you to have a job. However, I would encourage you even more strongly to start your own business, build it, and grow it. When you work for someone else, you are building someone else's dream. When you work for yourself, you are building your own dream.

For most people, a paycheck job is a steppingstone along the way, so just remember these two reasons why you are there: to learn more and to build capital.

3. THE TEACHING STAGE

You have done the work. You now have fruit on the tree. Now you get to walk the talk. It's time to share your success with others. Once you have gained expertise and experience, your next step is to share it with others.

It is during this stage that you begin to enjoy the fruits of your labor. Inspire others, teach them what you went through, and encourage them. Make a difference in their lives by sharing with them the secrets to your own success.

There are many ways to do this. You can write a book or teach a course. You can coach, mentor, or volunteer. Do what you are inspired to do to spread the good news of your success so that others may do the same and become successful too.

Once you have done this, you have completed the Cycle of Success. It doesn't matter whether it is done on a small scale or a big scale. What is important is that you have completed the cycle.

As you enjoy doing this stage in your journey to success, you will also find that success breeds success. The more you share your success with others, the more you become successful. What is even more amazing is that after sharing your success with others, you begin to realize that you need to learn even more. The more you learn, the more you want to learn and do. And the more you want to share. And so on.

The cycle continues.

PAY IT FORWARD

When you teach others, you're paying it forward. You are inspiring others to become successful by teaching them to do what you've done.

I believe everyone dreams of becoming successful in life. However, most people don't know how to go about it. Let me give you hope. As I quoted earlier, the very famous author, Napoleon Hill, in his classic success book *Think and Grow Rich* said: "Whatever the mind of man can conceive and believe, it can achieve."

Focus on your dream and follow the Cycle of Success. Make it your own personal success formula. Whatever it is that keeps burning deep inside you and keeps you going every day, hang on to it—because it can come true. Believe in your dream and find someone, maybe a coach or mentor, to help you achieve it.

And when you have achieved your dream, share your success story with others, so they will be inspired to do the same. Yes, pay it forward. This is the best way to live a purpose-driven and meaningful life.

CHAPTER 14

The Three Levels of Commitment

What is commitment? It is a decision to do something and to see it through. It is the determination to stick with your plans no matter what. And it is the resolve to never give up on your dreams. When you are committed to something, you are fully dedicated to achieving it. You are willing to do whatever it takes, and you are not afraid of hard work.

Why is commitment so important? Because without it, you will never reach your goals. A lack of commitment means that you are not willing to put in the hard work required to reach success. And it means that you are not willing to make the necessary sacrifices. You may have the best intentions, but if you are not committed to seeing them through, you will get derailed ... and eventually give up.

Commitment is important because it drives you to push through when things get tough. It is the glue that holds your dreams and aspirations together. It is what helps you stay focused on your goals, and it is what ultimately leads you to success. No matter what life throws your way, if you have a strong commitment to achieving your goals, you can overcome any obstacle.

With a strong commitment, anything is possible. You can achieve anything you set your mind to, as long as you are willing to work for it. So, if you want to achieve your goals, then you need to be committed to them. You need to have the determination to see them through, no matter what. And you need to be willing to make the necessary sacrifices. If you can do that, then you will be successful.

THE THREE LEVELS OF COMMITMENT

There are three different levels of commitment:

1. *"I will try."*
2. *"I will do my best."*
3. *"I will do whatever it takes."*

The level of commitment you choose will determine whether you are going to succeed or not in whatever it is that you have set out to do in life. Take your New Year's resolution for example. Is it to study more, to learn more, to lose weight, to lead more, to be a better father or mother, to be a better son or daughter, or simply to be a better person?

Whatever it is that you promised yourself you would do on the first day of the year, you need a certain level of commitment to fulfill that promise. Every January, millions of people resolve to get more fit, and they flock to gyms and sign up for memberships. By February, nearly all of them have stopped attending. You need to do more than try, more than intend, more than resolve.

1. *"I will try."*

How many times have you heard people saying that to you? Maybe you have said it to yourself. But what do we really mean when we say, "I will try"?

Based on my own experience, every time I hear people say to me, "I will try," I don't expect anything at all because they never do it. For so many years, I have heard this phrase, and yet I don't think people really know exactly what it does to our subconscious.

Even motivational speakers fall into this trap when they encourage their audience to *keep trying, keep trying.* Well, good luck with that. If you just keep trying, that's all you'll have. Trying is like practice. It's great training, but at some point, you need to get in the game. Unless you start doing, nothing happens.

Do you remember what Master Yoda said in the original *Star Wars* movie? He said, "It's either do or die; there is no try." From now on, don't just try doing it; do it.

2. *"I will do my best."*

I can almost imagine the sincere look on your face when you say this phrase. Very often we tell ourselves we will achieve this level of commitment, and we actually think we have made it. But when we realize that we did not quite make it, we make all kinds of excuses and say, "I did my best, but I guess my best wasn't good enough." After that, we tell ourselves, "What can I do, I'm only human." Unless you get rid of this kind of attitude, you will never be able to achieve your dreams.

3. *"I will do whatever it takes."*

Unless you have this highest level of commitment, you're only fooling yourself. You need to tell yourself that you are going to do whatever it takes. Whether you have a good day or a bad day, you need to do what you said you are going to do for that day. Whether it's raining or the sun is shining, you need to go because you said you're going. You must honor your commitment. Do whatever it takes. That's the only way you can become successful.

HOW CAN YOU APPLY THE THREE LEVELS OF COMMITMENT TO YOUR LIFE?

Let me explain the three levels of commitment in a more practical manner:

Level One is when you are only mildly interested in something and are not willing to exert much effort. This is curiosity but it doesn't move the needle. **Level Two** is when you are interested in something and are willing to put forth some effort. This is being half-assed or half-hearted. It's lackluster. Only at **Level Three** have you become so interested, so intrigued, so inspired that you are willing to do whatever you need to achieve your goal.

Let's look at some specific examples of these levels of commitment.

EXAMPLE 1: WHAT IS YOUR COMMITMENT TO GET A NEW SHIRT?

Level One commitment would be if you are mildly interested in getting a new shirt, but you're not willing to go out of your way or spend much money on it. You may be searching online, putting shirts in your cart, but you never get out your credit card.

Level Two commitment would be if you are interested in getting a new shirt and are willing to go out of your way but only if you can find a good price on it, quickly.

Level Three commitment would be if you are very interested in getting a new shirt, you really want the right shirt, and you are willing to spend a lot of money on it and go out of your way to find the perfect one. It may take a little longer, but it will be worth it.

EXAMPLE 2: WHAT IS YOUR COMMITMENT TO BUILD A GOOD RELATIONSHIP?

Level One commitment in a relationship would be if you are only mildly interested in the person and are not willing to do much to make the relationship work. They need to initiate. They need to always come to you and put you first. It has to be convenient.

Level Two commitment would be if you are interested in the person and are willing to do a little bit to make the relationship work, such as compromising or spending time with them.

Level Three commitment would be if you are very interested in the person and are willing to do a lot to make the relationship work, such as moving in with them, marrying them, or moving across the country for them.

EXAMPLE 3: WHAT IS YOUR COMMITMENT TO GET A JOB AND KEEP IT?

Level One commitment in a job would be if you are only mildly interested in the position and not willing to do much to keep it.

Level Two commitment would mean you are interested in the job and are willing to do a little bit to keep it, such as putting in extra hours or going above and beyond your job duties.

Level Three commitment would be if you are very interested in the job and are willing to do a lot to keep it, such as traveling to support the company or moving across the country for it.

EXAMPLE 4: WHAT IS YOUR COMMITMENT TO GET A GOOD EDUCATION?

Level One commitment would be if you are only mildly interested in getting a degree and are not willing to do much to make it happen.

Level Two commitment would be if you are interested in getting a degree and are willing to do a little bit to make it happen, such as attending classes most of the time and doing your homework.

Level Three commitment would be if you are very interested in getting a degree and are willing to do a lot to make it happen, such as sacrificing time with friends and family to study or relocating to the best school. It's a high priority in your life.

Commitment is a decision. It's a choice to be there, to do the best you can, and to follow through. It takes determination to see things through, no matter what. It means you're in it for the long haul no matter what obstacles get in your way. It means you're serious about your relationships, your work, your dreams—everything in your life. When you make a commitment, you're saying, "I am all in."

When it comes to relationships, making a commitment is pledging to be there for your partner through thick and thin. It's vowing to always be honest and open no matter what. It's promising to support them no matter what they do and be their biggest cheerleader. By making a commitment, you are telling your partner that you are firmly in the relationship for the long haul. And that is a powerful thing.

In the workplace, making a commitment means dedicating yourself to your job and doing your best every day. It means being on time, meeting deadlines and following through on your commitments. It means being reliable and trustworthy.

> *Commitment is a powerful thing. Don't take it for granted.*

When it comes to your dreams, making a commitment means doing whatever it takes to achieve them. It means sacrificing time and energy and never giving up. It means staying the course no matter what. So, what does commitment mean to you? What are you all in for?

CHAPTER 15

The Principle of Self-Discipline

Self-discipline is the ability to regulate one's behavior to achieve a goal. It is one of the most important principles for pursuing a better life because it allows you to control your own actions, instead of being controlled by your impulses or emotions. A self-disciplined person sets goals and achieves them despite any obstacles or distractions that may come in their way.

Self-discipline is one of the most important traits a person can have. It's the ability to do what you should do, when you should do it, whether you feel like it or not. This includes things like getting up early in the morning, going to bed on time, eating healthy, and exercising consistently.

Self-discipline is essential for achieving any kind of success. It allows you to stay focused and motivated, even when things get tough. It also helps you stay consistent, which is key for achieving long-term goals. And finally, self-discipline enables you to resist temptation and overcome bad habits, which can hold you back from reaching your potential.

So, if you want to achieve anything in life, you need to develop a strong sense of self-discipline. It may not be easy, but it's definitely worth the effort. Just remember to take things one step at a time, and don't give up when things get tough. With a little perseverance, you can achieve anything you set your mind to.

When you have self-discipline, you're able to accomplish more and achieve your goals. You're also less likely to succumb to temptation or give up when things get tough.

Developing self-discipline is one of the most important things you can do for yourself. It's what allows you to live a better life.

HERE ARE SOME TIPS ON SELF-DISCIPLINE:

1. *Make a plan and stick to it.*

   If you have a goal, create a plan of action that will help you achieve it. Breaking your goal down into smaller steps will make it seem less daunting and will make it easier to track your progress.

2. *Set deadlines for yourself.*

   When you have a timeline for completing a task, it's easier to stay on track.

3. *Find a support group.*

   If you have others who are also working toward developing self-discipline, it will be easier to stay consistent.

4. *Hold yourself accountable.*

   Write down your goals and review them often. This will help you make sure you're making progress.

5. *Reward yourself for your accomplishments.*

   Celebrate each accomplishment, no matter how small, with a special treat or activity that you enjoy.

Developing self-discipline is not easy, but it's definitely worth it. When you have self-discipline, you're able to achieve your goals and be successful in anything you do. It is the key to success.

If you can master your own mind and body, you can achieve anything you want in life. It's all about having the willpower to go the distance, despite temptations and distractions.

Self-discipline requires planning and organization. You need to develop good habits and stick to them while avoiding bad habits. This can be challenging, but it's worth it in the end. Self-discipline is also about being able to control your emotions. You need to be able to stay calm and focused when things get tough. This takes practice, but it's definitely achievable with a bit of effort.

So, if you want to achieve your goals, start by working on your self-discipline. It's the key to success!

SECTION FOUR

Levels of EXCELLENCE

CHAPTER 16

The Secret of Fulfillment is Excellence

Excellence is defined as "the quality of being excellent." It is a word that is often used but not always understood. To be excellent is to be better than average, to be outstanding.

But what does that mean for you? What does it mean for your business? What does it mean for your life?

For me, it means striving for the best. It means doing what I do the best way that I can possibly do it. It means setting high standards and meeting them every time. It means being the best version of myself.

For my business, it means delivering the best product or service possible. It means going above and beyond what is expected. It means being the best in my industry.

Excellence is not easy. It takes hard work and dedication. But it is worth it. When you are excellent, you stand out from the crowd. You shine brightly. You make a difference.

The secret of fulfillment is excellence. You must be excellent in everything you do. There is no other way to be happy and fulfilled in life. You must set the highest standards for yourself and then exceed them. Only then will you find true happiness and fulfillment in life. Pursue excellence in everything you do, and you will find the path to true fulfillment.

HOW DO YOU ACHIEVE EXCELLENCE IN YOUR LIFE?

There is no simple answer, but one key is to always aim high. Don't be content with mediocrity. Strive for excellence in everything you do and never give up.

Another key is to learn from your mistakes. Nobody is perfect, and you will make mistakes. But if you learn from your mistakes, you will get closer to excellence.

Finally, surround yourself with positive people who will encourage you to reach your goals. Nobody can achieve excellence on their own, so find people who will help you become the best version of yourself. They will cheer you on and celebrate your successes, yes, but they will also nudge you, coax you, cajole you, and give you a kick in the you-know-what when you need one!

WHY STRIVE FOR EXCELLENCE?

Excellence is a pursuit that is unique to everyone. For some it may be reaching the pinnacle of their field or becoming the best at what they do. For others, it may mean making a difference in the lives of others or becoming the best possible version of themselves. No matter how you define excellence, there are a few common reasons why striving for excellence is a worthwhile pursuit.

First, excellence enables you to achieve more than you even thought possible. When you set your sights high and continually strive to improve, you find ways to do things you never thought you could do. This applies to both your personal and professional life.

Second, excellence leads to greater happiness and fulfillment. When you are constantly challenging yourself and pushing yourself to be your best, you find more satisfaction and happiness in what you do.

Finally, excellence makes a positive impact on those around you. When you are always striving to be your best, it inspires them to do the same. This can have a positive effect on your relationships, your community, and even the world at large.

Achieving excellence is not easy, but it is worth it. When you reach the pinnacle of your field, you will be proud of what you have accomplished. So don't give up. Keep striving for excellence in your life!

WHAT ARE THE LEVELS OF EXCELLENCE?

There is no one definition of excellence because it can mean different things to different people. However, there are some general levels of excellence that everyone can strive for.

The first level of excellence is simply *doing your best*. This may not be the highest level of achievement, but it's a good starting point. If you do your best, you're giving it your best effort, and you can be proud of that.

The next level of excellence is *setting high standards* for yourself and always aiming to improve. You may not always reach your goals, but by setting the bar high, you're always pushing yourself to do better.

Always strive for the next level of excellence in your chosen field. If you're a musician, strive for excellence in your music. If you're a painter, aim to create the best paintings possible. Whatever your chosen field, strive to be the best at it.

The final level of excellence is becoming a *master of your craft*. This is the highest level of achievement, and it's only possible if you devote your life to your craft. Once you reach this level, you're the best at what you do, and there's no one who can touch you.

So, what's your definition of excellence? What level are you striving for? Whatever your definition, always aim to do your best and push yourself to reach new heights.

HOW DO YOU PREPARE YOURSELF TO ACHIEVE EXCELLENCE?

There is no simple path to success. It takes hard work, dedication, and a willingness to put in the effort required to be the best. But it's possible. Here are a few tips to help you on your way:

1. *Set your goals high and be realistic about what you can achieve.*

    Shoot for the stars but know that there is always room for improvement.

2. *Be passionate about what you do.*

    When you love what you're doing, work becomes less of a chore and more of a pleasure.

3. *Practice, practice, practice.*

    The only way to get better at something is to do it repeatedly.

4. *Take care of yourself both physically and mentally.*

    You can't expect to do your best if you're not feeling your best.

5. *Surround yourself with positive people.*

These maybe your friends and family who will support your efforts and encourage you to keep reaching for the top.

It's easy to get bogged down by life's challenges and let our dreams of excellence fade away. But it's important to remember that we are capable of so much more than we give ourselves credit for. With hard work, practice, and a little bit of passion, we can all achieve greatness. So don't be afraid to shoot for the stars because you never know what might be possible.

TO DO SOMETHING WELL IS TO ENJOY IT.

It is often said that to do something well is to enjoy it. And I believe this is true. When you do something you love, it doesn't feel like work—it feels like joy.

I consider myself an excellent musician. I play the piano, guitar, bass, and drums. I love to play music; it is a huge part of my life. I have been playing music for many years. I am always looking for new ways to become a better musician. I am very passionate about music, and I love to share my music with others. I have performed in front of small and large audiences. I love the feeling of being on stage and playing music for people.

I believe that music is one of the most important experiences in life. It can bring joy to people, and it can also be used to communicate emotions and ideas. I am grateful for the gift of music, and I will continue to use it to make the world a better place. I have worked hard to achieve this level of excellence and it has paid off. I am so grateful to God for all my accomplishments, and I know that He will always guide me so I can continue to be the best at what I do.

Whenever someone asks me what I do for a living, I love being able to say that I am a music teacher. It's something that I am truly excellent at. I've been doing it for more than forty years, and I know that I'm making a difference in the lives of my students. It wasn't always easy. I put in a lot of hard work and dedication. But it was worth it. Because now, I can look back and say that I was truly excellent at what I did. Every day, I get to witness the joy that music brings to people's lives. And that is truly a gift.

> *Striving for excellence is a continuous process. It's an ongoing journey that never really ends.*

Every day we should aim to do our best and learn as much as possible. There's always something new to learn, and we can always get better. When we reach for excellence, we're setting the bar high for ourselves and pushing ourselves to be our best. And that's a good thing. We all make mistakes, but what matters is how we learn from them. We can't be afraid to try new things and challenge ourselves. That's the only way we'll grow and improve. So, let's all strive for excellence and see what we can achieve. Becoming excellent takes a lot of time and effort, but it is definitely worth it in the end.

HOW DO I ACHIEVE EXCELLENCE IN WHAT I DO?

Some people seem to be born with a natural talent for excellence. But for most of us, excellence is something we have to work for. Here are a few tips I want to share with you that I personally used for achieving excellence and fulfillment in my career:

1. *I set high standards and strive to exceed them.*

2. *I make the highest level of commitment to continuous learning and self-improvement.*

3. *I pay attention to details and take pride in my work.*

4. *I am patient and persistent in my efforts.*

5. *I surround myself with positive people who support my vision and my actions.*

I hope that you, too, can find an activity you love, something that brings you joy and makes you feel alive. Because when you do, you'll know you're on the right path, the path to excellence.

CHAPTER 17

Understanding and Overcoming the Fear of Failure

Failure is not a destination; it's a step on the way to success. It is an opportunity to learn and grow. Some people avoid failure at all costs, but if you want to be successful, you must be willing to fail. Failing is part of the journey. It is an inevitable part of life. We all make mistakes, but it's how we learn from them that determines our success. When you view failure as an opportunity to learn and grow, you'll be unstoppable. But how do you understand failure? One way to understand failure is to ask yourself: What did I learn from this experience? Did I learn something new about myself or my business? Did I make a mistake that I can learn from? What can I do differently next time? If you can learn from your failures, you'll be one step closer to success.

WHAT IS FEAR?

Fear is a feeling that people experience when they are in danger or when they think they might be in danger. Fear can make people feel scared, anxious, or worried. Some people might feel like they need to run away or hide.

There are different types of fear. Some people might be afraid of things like spiders or snakes. Other people might be afraid of public speaking or getting surgery.

Fear can be a normal reaction to a dangerous situation. However, sometimes people can feel too afraid to do things that they want to do or that are important to them. This is called an anxiety disorder. If you are feeling afraid or anxious a lot of the time, it might be helpful to talk to a therapist or psychologist. They can help you understand your fear and find ways to manage it.

There are some techniques that can help you deal with fear. One of these is called exposure therapy. This involves exposing you to the things you are afraid of in small doses. This can help you learn that the thing that you are afraid of is not as bad as you thought it was. I suggest that you have professional support for this.

WHAT IS FEAR OF FAILURE?

Fear of failure is the fear of not being successful. People who experience fear of failure often have a fear of not being able to do something right or of not being able to meet someone's expectations. This kind of fear can lead to anxiety and stress, which can then interfere with their ability to perform well, in a negative spiral. There are a few different ways to deal with fear of failure. One is with exposure therapy, as I mentioned earlier. This can help you become more comfortable with your fears and increase your confidence. Another approach is to accept that failure is a part of life and isn't necessarily a bad thing. It can help you learn and grow from your experiences.

Finally, it's important to have a good support system in place, whether that be friends, family, or a therapist. These people can help you during times of difficulty and provide encouragement when you need it. If you're struggling with fear of failure, it's important to get help. Talk to someone you trust about your feelings and seek out therapy if needed. With the right tools, you can overcome your fear and start thriving in all aspects of your life.

HOW CAN I UNDERSTAND FEAR OF FAILURE?

One way to understand fear of failure is to think of it as the fear of not being able to meet your own expectations. This fear can be paralyzing and can keep you from trying new things or taking risks.

I pointed out earlier that there are several ways to overcome fear of failure, but the most important thing is to have a clear understanding of your own strengths and weaknesses. Once you know where you stand, you can start taking steps to improve your skills in areas where you are weak.

Personally, I overcome my own fear of failure by having a positive attitude. I believe in myself and my ability to succeed. When I approach new challenges with confidence, the fear of failure will be less likely to hold me back. I learned that failure is a part of life. Everyone makes mistakes, and the key is to learn from them and move on. I don't let fear of failure keep me from living my life to the fullest.

WHAT ARE PEOPLE AFRAID OF?

What are the main causes of fear of failure? Studies have shown that there are many different reasons why people are afraid of failure. Some of the most common causes include a fear of not being good enough, a fear of not being able to achieve one's goals, and a fear of disappointing others. Some people may also be afraid of the consequences that failure may have, such as embarrassment, humiliation, or even financial ruin. Other people may simply be afraid of the sensation of failure itself, which can be incredibly discouraging and demoralizing.

Whatever the reason, it's important to understand that fear of failure can be a major obstacle in achieving success. If you are afraid of failure, it's important to take some time to reflect on why this is.

What is your main fear? What are the consequences of failure for you? Once you have a better understanding of why you are afraid of failure, you can start to come up with strategies to overcome this fear.

WHAT ARE THE CAUSES OF FEAR OF FAILURE?

Fear of failure is a very common psychological condition that can affect people of any age. Some of the most common causes of fear of failure are:

1. ***Perfectionism.***

    This is one of the most common causes of fear of failure. People who are perfectionists often set extremely high standards for themselves, and they are never satisfied with their own achievements. This can lead to a lot of anxiety and stress, and it can make it difficult to take risks or try new things.

2. ***Anxiety and depression.***

    These are two mental health conditions that can also contribute to fear of failure. People who suffer from anxiety or depression often feel like they are not good enough and that they can't succeed. This can lead to a lot of self-doubt and hesitation, which can prevent them from achieving their goals.

3. ***Lack of self-confidence.***

    Another common factor that contributes to fear of failure is a lack of self-confidence. People who don't believe in themselves often don't believe that they can succeed at anything. This can prevent them from trying new things and taking risks, which can lead to a lot of disappointment and frustration.

4. *Negative thinking.*

People who have a negative outlook on life often expect the worst to happen. This can lead to a lot of anxiety and stress, which makes it difficult to take risks or challenges.

5. *Previous failures.*

People who have failed in the past may be afraid of failing again. The mere thought of taking another risky endeavor frightens people who have experienced failure in their previous undertakings.

6. *Fear of the unknown.*

People who are afraid of the unknown may be afraid of failing because they don't know what will happen if they don't succeed, or even if they do.

Whatever the reason, it is very obvious that fear of failure can be a major obstacle to achieving success. It can lead to procrastination and hesitation and can prevent people from taking risks or trying new things. This can ultimately lead to a loss of opportunities and a lower quality of life. However, I have good news for you. There are ways how to overcome the fear of failure. You can start all over again and this time, you will succeed because you have already learned your lesson. Keep reading.

HOW DO I OVERCOME THE FEAR OF FAILURE?

One way to overcome fear of failure is to develop a growth mindset. This means believing that you can improve and learn from your failures. When you approach failures in this way, they become less scary and more helpful in learning how to become successful. Another way to overcome fear of failure is to set realistic goals for yourself. Don't try to achieve things that are beyond your ability.

There are several ways to overcome fear of failure. Here's some of them:

1. ***Aim for excellence instead of perfection.***

    When you strive for excellence, you are constantly bettering yourself and expanding what you can achieve. If you aim for perfection, you will always be disappointed because no one is perfect; everyone makes mistakes.

2. ***Build self-confidence.***

    If you lack confidence, try taking some steps to improve your self-esteem. This can help you feel more confident and less afraid of failing.

3. ***Challenge yourself.***

    Challenging yourself can help you become more comfortable with taking risks.

4. *Learn to accept failure as a natural part of life.*

It is important to remember that failure is not a reflection on your worth as a person. You can also practice self-compassion and forgive yourself when things do not go as planned.

5. *Set realistic goals.*

It is important to have goals that challenge you, but they should also be achievable. When you set goals that are too lofty, you are more likely to become discouraged and give up if you do not reach them.

6. *Have a support system in place.*

This can include family, friends, or a trusted mentor. They can encourage you when things get tough and can provide a listening ear when you need to talk about your struggles.

CHAPTER 18

The Ladder to Excellence

There is no substitute for hard work. You have to put in the hours if you want to achieve excellence in any field. But what if there were a shortcut? There is. It's called the ladder to excellence. And it's a process you can use to speed up your journey to the top.

The ladder to excellence is simple. You start by learning as much as you can about your chosen subject. Then you put that knowledge into practice, refining your skills until you reach the top of your game. It won't be easy, but it will be worth it. The rewards of excellence are many: respect, admiration, and even financial success. Excellence is a continuous journey. It's not a destination that you reach and then you're done.

It's a constant quest to become the best you can be. Each day you need to work on improving yourself in some way. So don't be content with being just good enough. Strive for excellence and let it take you to new heights.

WHAT ARE THE STEPS TO BECOME EXCELLENT IN WHAT YOU DO?

Becoming excellent at anything takes time, focus, and effort. Here are the steps that you need to take to achieve excellence in whatever you do:

1. Determine what you want to be excellent at. This may not be easy, but it is important to be clear about what you want to achieve.

2. Research and learn everything you can about the subject. Become an expert in your field.

3. Practice, practice, practice. This is how you will improve and become better at what you do.

4. Set high standards for yourself and always strive to reach them.

5. Be patient and never give up on your goal of excellence. It takes time and hard work to achieve greatness, but it is worth it in the end.

Let me explain further each step in the ladder to excellence.

1. DETERMINE WHAT YOU WANT TO EXCEL AT.

Most people want to excel at everything, but that's not realistic. Choose one area in your life where you want to be excellent and focus your efforts there. What area should you focus on? That depends on what you want to accomplish. If you want to be an excellent parent, then focus on becoming a good role model for your children. If you want to be an excellent employee, then focus on developing strong work habits and becoming a team player.

No matter what you choose, always remember that excellence is a journey not a destination. It can be anything from your job to your relationships to your physical health. Identify what it takes to be excellent in that area and begin taking small steps toward reaching that goal. It can be difficult to know where to start when it comes to becoming excellent at something. But by focusing your efforts and breaking down the task into manageable steps, you can make progress toward your goal.

2. RESEARCH THE SUBJECT IN WHICH YOU WANT TO EXCEL.

After you have chosen the area in which you want to excel, find out what it takes to be excellent in that area. What skills do you need to develop? What habits do you need to adopt? What attitudes do you need to cultivate? Do comprehensive research and learn everything you can about that area. Once you know what you need to do, begin by taking small steps toward reaching that goal.

There will be setbacks and challenges along the way, but don't let them discourage you. Continue striving toward excellence and eventually you will reach your goal. Remember, *it's not about perfection; it's about progress.* So, keep moving forward and eventually you will achieve excellence in whatever area you choose.

It can be difficult to know where to start on the ladder to excellence. That's where a coach or mentor can help. A mentor or coach can help you on your path to achieving excellence in your field. A good mentor can give you the knowledge and advice you need to get ahead. A good coach can help you develop the skills you need to be successful. If you're serious about achieving excellence in your field, then don't hesitate to get a mentor or coach. It can make all the difference in the world.

3. *PRACTICE, PRACTICE, PRACTICE*

Repetition is the mother of skill. To achieve excellence in anything, you must practice. This is especially true, for example, for people who have decided to learn a musical instrument. You can't expect to be a world-class musician without practicing every day. Submit yourself to a music teacher, an expert, who can help and guide you as you practice and work your way up the ladder to excellence.

Practice makes perfect, so be sure to put in the effort and you will be rewarded with success. The same is true for other skills, such as cooking, athletics, and art. You have to put in the time if you want to be the best. Of course, practice isn't easy. It's often boring and tedious. But it's worth it because the more you practice, the better you'll become. Practice, practice, practice until you get it right; keep on practicing until you'll never get it wrong.

Here are a few tips how to practice:

1. Set aside time to practice.
2. Make a commitment to yourself to improve your skills.
3. Practice with a purpose, focusing on your goals.
4. Review your progress and re-assess.
5. Be patient and never give up.

The ladder to excellence is a journey that requires dedication and hard work.

It starts with commitment, diligence, and action. With discipline and determination, you can reach the top of the ladder and achieve excellence.

4. SET HIGH STANDARDS FOR YOURSELF AND ALWAYS STRIVE TO REACH THEM.

It's important to have high standards for yourself and always strive to reach them. This is a very important rung in the ladder to excellence. By setting high standards, you'll push yourself to achieve more than you ever thought possible. Just make sure that your standards are achievable and realistic; don't set yourself up for failure by setting unrealistic goals.

There is no end to the pursuit of excellence. Once you've reached your goals, set new ones, and keep pushing yourself higher. As you strive for excellence, you'll climb the ladder to success. However, reaching the top of the ladder is only the beginning. To be truly excellent, you must continue to pursue ever higher goals. There is no limit to what you can do. So, keep climbing, and one day you'll reach the pinnacle of success.

5. BE PATIENT AND NEVER GIVE UP ON YOUR GOAL OF EXCELLENCE.

The ladder to excellence is a long and arduous journey. But it's a journey that is worth making because at the end of the ladder lies a world of opportunity.

The first step on the ladder is to set your goals. You need to have a clear idea of what you want to achieve, and you need to be motivated to accomplish those goals. Without motivation, you'll never make it to the top of the ladder.

The second step is to develop a plan of action. You need to have a roadmap that will help you reach your goals. This includes setting deadlines and milestones and creating a timeline for your progress.

The third step is to take action. This is where the rubber meets the road, and where you put your plan into action. You need to be willing to work hard and persevere through the challenges.

The last step is to stay focused. It's easy to get sidetracked when you're working toward a goal, but you need to stay focused on what's important. It is filled with hard work, dedication, and perseverance. However, the rewards are worth the effort. The journey begins with a single step, and it is up to you to take that step. Be patient and never give up on your goal. With hard work and determination, you will reach the top of the ladder to excellence.

CHAPTER 19

The Best Pathway To Success

We all want the people we care about to share in our happiness and success. However, it's important to remember that what works for one person may not work for another. You must find your own pathway to success and happiness. There is no single path that is guaranteed to work for everyone. There are many different paths you can take, and it's up to you to find the one that works best for you.

FIND YOUR OWN PERSONAL SUCCESS FORMULA.

One of the most important things to find is your own personal success formula. You need to find what makes you happy and what helps you achieve your goals. There are plenty of resources—books, articles, websites, coaches, and mentors—out there to help you figure out what works best for you.

Don't be afraid to try new things; it can be a great way to learn and grow. Remember, you won't always succeed at everything you do—and that's okay. You can learn from your mistakes. Be creative and have fun! Be open to change and willing to adapt as needed. The most successful people are those who are constantly learning and evolving. Don't be afraid to change course if you find that something isn't working for you.

In the beginning, it's tough to see the progress you're making. You might feel like you're stuck and that you're not getting anywhere. But remember, Rome wasn't built in a day. It takes time and effort to achieve your goals. Don't get discouraged if you don't see results right away. Keep working hard and stay focused on your goals. Eventually, you'll start to see progress and will be one step closer to achieving your dreams. The path to success is not always easy, but it's definitely worth it.

Setbacks are inevitable, but don't let them discourage you. Every successful person has faced failure along the way. Learning from your mistakes and picking yourself up after a fall is what makes you stronger and better prepared for future success.

It's important to remember that progress doesn't come easy. It will take hard work, determination, and a lot of resilience. Once you start moving forward, however, it's important to keep your eyes peeled for the signs that you're slipping, and to stay focused on the goalposts. It's through these hard times that you'll ultimately reach your destination.

Whatever path you choose, make sure to stay focused and motivated. Keep your eyes on the prize and don't give up when things get tough. Keep working toward your goals, and you'll eventually reach them. With hard work and dedication, you can achieve anything you set your mind to.

FIND THE RIGHT BALANCE.

There is a fine line between taking on a challenge and overdoing it. As the saying goes "haste makes waste." On one hand, we may feel that if we don't take on every opportunity that comes our way, we'll miss out on something great. On the other hand, we may feel that if we take on too many challenges at once, we'll just end up burned out.

Many of us tend to feel frustrated when trying to live up to our ideals. However, the fact is if you set your goals high and make sure to stay motivated, anything is possible. Remember that the journey to success isn't always a smooth one.

It's important to find the right balance for ourselves. We need to be willing to take on new challenges but also be realistic about what we can handle. If we're not careful, we can easily overdo it and end up feeling frustrated and stressed.

So how do we find that balance? It's not always easy, but here are a few tips:

1. *Evaluate your current situation.*

   What are your strengths and weaknesses? What are you currently working on?

2. *Make a plan.*

   Decide what you want to achieve and create a roadmap to get there.

3. *Take small steps.*

   You don't need to do everything at once. Break down big goals into smaller, more manageable tasks.

4. *Ask for help when you need it.*

   Don't be afraid to reach out to others for advice or support.

5. *Celebrate your successes!*

   Give yourself credit for all the progress you've made.

Finding the right balance can be challenging, but it's worth it in the end. When we're able to find a healthy balance for ourselves, we're able to accomplish more and feel happier and more fulfilled.

Live an honest and ethical lifestyle.

There are a variety of methods and strategies you can use to achieve your goal. One common thread in all of them is honesty and ethical living (in words, thoughts, and actions) pertaining to your lifestyle.

Moral and ethical standards in any business ranks highest and should not be overlooked. The only way to achieve a healthy life-work balance after gaining great wealth is to maintain the true essence of life. This is where the importance of maintaining high moral and ethical standards come into play. You may have all the money in the world, but if you don't have a good sense of morality and ethics, you will not be happy. Money cannot buy happiness. Happiness can only be found by living a life of giving back to others.

One way to maintain such high standards is to always act with integrity. This means doing the right thing even when no one is watching. It also means being honest and truthful in all your dealings. Acting with integrity is one of the most important things you can do to maintain your moral compass.

Another way to maintain high moral and ethical standards is to be charitable. Giving back to the community is a great way to show that you care about others and that you are willing to help those in need. Charitable giving also helps to improve your own life by making you feel happier and more fulfilled.

Finally, it is important to remember that there are many ways to maintain high standards. What works for one person might not work for another, so it is important to find the approach that works best for you and stick to it.

If you're looking for the best pathway to success, look no further. The following tips will help you achieve your dreams and goals:

1. *Believe in yourself.*

    You must believe in yourself if you want to achieve anything in life. If you don't think you can do it, then you never will. Have confidence in yourself and your abilities and remember that you are in control of your own destiny.

2. *Set goals and plan.*

    If you don't have any goals, it's going to be difficult to achieve success. You need to set goals and make a plan of action on how you're going to reach those goals. Having a clear path to success will help keep you motivated and on track.

3. *Stay focused and don't give up.*

   To be successful, you must stay focused and never give up. There will be times when things get tough, and you'll want to give up, but don't let that stop you. Persevere and keep moving forward.

4. *Take action and don't be afraid to fail.*

   Success doesn't come easy; you must be willing to act and risk failure. Don't be afraid to make mistakes because it's through those mistakes that you'll learn and grow. Be fearless in your pursuit of success.

CHAPTER 20

Maximizing Your God-Given Gifts

We all have a gift. We may not realize it but each of us has been given a gift by God. It doesn't matter whether our gift is small or great; the important thing is that we have a gift or even multiple gifts.

HAVE YOU IDENTIFIED YOUR GIFT YET?

If you have, fantastic and congratulations. If you haven't, it's okay. After reading this chapter, it's quite likely that not only will you be able to recognize your God-given gift, but you will also learn how to maximize it.

Experts in psychology say that 50 percent of who we are is attributed to the genes we inherited from our parents. The other

50 percent depends on what we make of these genes. This is the reason why there are people who are born with talents. What they are actually saying is that if your father or mother is a musician, you will probably have the same talent when you grow up. I personally believe this is true. But having the innate talent does not make you a great musician.

In this chapter, I will show you what you need to do with the other 50 percent of your makeup so you can maximize the talents that you inherited from your parents. And don't try to sell me the idea that you don't have any talents at all. I won't buy that. So, sit tight and get ready for a profoundly serious yet fun and revealing journey of how you can maximize your God-given gift(s).

HOW DO YOU FIND YOUR GIFT?

One common method in discovering and identifying your gift is self-assessment. To do this, ask yourself these three questions:

1. If you are not working at a job the following day, what is it that gets you up early in the morning and keeps you up late at night?

2. What is it that when you are doing it, you lose track of time, forget to eat, and are inspired and filled with joy while doing it?

3. What is it that when you are doing it, you feel like it's just natural for you to do it without much effort or struggle?

Your answer to the three questions is your gift.

Another common method in discovering and identifying your gift is to ask someone, perhaps a friend, close family member, or relative what they think your gift is. Why? Because in most cases, these people are our number one critics and also our fans. They will usually give you their honest opinion. For example, if you want to find out whether you have a talent in, say, singing, ask them after you sing. (If you are not satisfied with any of their opinions, you can always go to a professional vocal music coach and let him or her pronounce the verdict.)

TALENTS YOU MAY ALREADY HAVE BUT HAVEN'T IDENTIFIED YET:

1. Artistic skill (painting, photography, sculpture, etc.)
2. Musical skill (composer, songwriter, singer, etc.)
3. Dancing skill (ballet, contemporary, ballroom, etc.)
4. Public speaking skill (orator, motivational, etc.)
5. Coaching skill (business, sports, life, executive, etc.)
6. Business skill (business intelligence, business planner, etc.)
7. Teaching skill (classroom, private, etc.)
8. Writing skill (book author, poet, song lyricist, etc.)
9. Athletic skill (tennis, swimming, marathon, etc.)
10. Cooking skill (master chef, food preparation, etc.)

> *Whatever your talent is, acknowledge that God has given it to you either genetically from your parents or through hard work and dedication.*

We all have God-given gifts. We are all unique, and we all have something special to offer. However, many of us never realize our potential because we don't know how to maximize our gifts.

TIPS TO HELP YOU UNLEASH THE POWER OF YOUR GIFTS:

1. Find your passion.

The first step is to find your passion. What do you love to do? What gets you excited? What do you feel you're called to do? When you find your passion, you will naturally start to use your gifts more effectively.

Your gifts are meant to be used for God's glory. When you find your passion and use your gifts to serve Him, you will be amazed at what He can do through you. As you continue to grow in your faith, you will be able to use your gifts more effectively. It is important to stay humble and keep God at the center of your life. Do not let your gifts go to your head. Remember that it is God who gives you these gifts, and He can take them away just as easily. Be thankful for the gifts that you have been given and use them to build up the kingdom of God.

The Bible tells us that we are all given different gifts by God. These gifts can be used to build up the kingdom of God and to help others. We should be thankful for the gifts we have been given and use them to make a difference in the world.

2. Set your goals.

Once you know your passion, set some goals for yourself. What do you want to achieve? What do you want to accomplish? What do you want to contribute? When you have goals, you will be more motivated to use your gifts in the best way possible.

Your gifts are given to you by God for a specific purpose. As you discover what your gifts are, you can begin to use them in the service of God and humanity. You have a unique combination of talents and abilities that can be used to make a difference in the world.

One way to maximize your gifts is by setting goals. When you have goals, you will be more motivated to use your gifts in the best way possible. You can set goals for yourself in different areas of your life, such as personal, professional, spiritual, or family-related goals. As you accomplish these goals, you will be able to see how God is using your gifts to make an impact in the world.

Another way to use your gifts to their fullest potential is by serving others. When you serve others, you are using your gifts in a way that benefits others. You can serve others through your work, through volunteerism, or through other means. As you serve others, you will see how your gifts can make a difference in the lives of others.

When you use your gifts in a way that honors God and benefits others, you are living out your purpose in life. As you continue to use your gifts in this way, you will see how God can use them to change the world.

3. Get trained.

One of the best ways to maximize your gifts is to get trained in what you love to do. Find a mentor or a teacher who can help you learn and grow in your chosen field. When you have the proper training, you will be able to use your gifts more effectively and reach your goals sooner. There is no one-size-fits-all answer to maximize your God-given gifts. It will vary depending on the gift itself. However, there are a few general tips that can help you make the most of whatever talents you have been blessed with. First, it is important to identify your gifts. This can be done by taking assessments, asking others who know you well, or doing some research on what you are naturally good at.

Once you have a good idea of what your gifts are, you need to develop them. Aim to use them as much as possible in your everyday life. This may mean finding a job or hobby that incorporates your strengths, getting trained in the area, or simply using your gifts to help others in whatever way you can.

Second, it is important to stay humble and grateful for your gifts. No matter how talented you may be, remember that God gave you these gifts for a reason and that you should use them to honor Him. Stay focused on using your gifts for good and be thankful for the opportunities God provides to do so. In a sense, if you fail to ever use your God-given gifts, you are rejecting a gift from God. Think about that.

Finally, never give up. It may take time and effort to fully maximize your God-given gifts, but it is definitely worth the effort. With hard work and dedication, you can use your gifts to make a difference in the world and bring glory to God.

4. Practice, practice, practice.

No matter how good you are at your talent or skill, you still need to practice. The more you practice, the better you will become. So, find a way to use your gifts regularly and get better at them. The sky is the limit!

SECTION FIVE

The Missions of LEADERSHIP

CHAPTER 21

The RIGHT Principles to Live By

In this chapter allow me to share with you five key principles that I am continuously striving to follow and live by as guideposts in my journey to pursue a better life.

These universal principles are the solid foundation in creating a code of ethics in your life. It is important to mention that living in accordance with moral values and following the laws of nature can lead you to a wholesome existence and a better life.

These key principles will help you unlock your potential to acquire wealth and abundance to live a better and successful life. These principles practically have a spiritual basis in which we all draw our true innate qualities.

These principles are:

- Respect
- Integrity
- Gratitude
- Honesty
- Trust

1. RESPECT

Respect is the key to a better life. It is the foundation that supports our relationships and productivity. It helps us understand and appreciate others. It allows us to weigh our consequences and make responsible decisions. Without respect, we are at a loss for what to do with our lives.

It is important to understand that respect is not a one-time event but rather a journey that will require time and effort. Developing a life of respect is a journey that starts with learning and understanding our obligations. It is a journey of learning to appreciate that we must learn to respect our friends, family, and colleagues. It is a journey of learning to make better choices in life. Most importantly, it is a journey of learning to respect ourselves.

There is no question that respect is necessary for a healthy, productive life. However, it is not the only required ingredient. It is important to have strong relationships and to be productive. Unfortunately, many people do not develop these relationships or are not productive because they do not develop respect for others.

To develop a life of respect, we must first develop a solid foundation. This foundation includes learning to understand our obligations and responsibilities toward other people as individuals and as members of a community.

There is also no question that respect is one of the most important values in a workplace.

Employees who respect each other help create a positive work environment in which everyone feels valued and appreciated. Their actions can set an example for the rest of the workplace and help build a more positive relationship with their employers as well as with the customers and clients served by the company.

Tips for being respectful in your workplace:

1. Be aware of your own behavior and how it may be perceived by those around you.
2. Be considerate of other people's time and space.
3. Respond graciously to all requests for assistance.
4. Be mindful of your employer's wishes and expectations.
5. Be conscientious of your words and actions.

One way in which you can start to practice the principle of respect in a business environment is by speaking out against unethical actions. This will show that you care about people and will help you make more responsible decisions. You can also work to build a healthy relationship with your customers. This will show that you care about their well-being and the satisfaction of their needs. You can also show maturity in your business by looking at every situation from a unique perspective. This way you will be able to make sound decisions that will benefit everyone.

2. INTEGRITY

Integrity means being honest, truthful, and reliable. Integrity is a fundamental principle in business and in life.

For a business, integrity is important because it helps ensure that the company's values are followed. Integrity should be a key focus of everyone on the team. Integrity fosters trust, and trust is the foundation of any great organization. When employees feel that their needs are being addressed and their feelings are being taken into consideration, they are more likely to stay with the company for a long period of time—a critical factor in keeping businesses running successfully.

Integrity is also important in your personal life. If you cheat on school exams, for example, that would hurt your reputation and could get you expelled. Likewise, if you were to lie to your friends, that would jeopardize your relationships.

One way to build integrity into your business is by learning and practicing the ABBs (Ambition, Belief, and Behavior). Ambition is the desire to achieve something great. Belief is the conviction that what you are doing is right and worthwhile. Behavior is the act of doing what you believe is best for all. All of these are examples of how integrity protects people and things.

To be a person of integrity, you must be honest, truthful, and reliable as much as you can, in every way.

3. GRATITUDE

One of the most important things people can do for their mental and physical health is to develop a sense of gratitude. Gratitude can help reduce anxiety, depression, and stress. It improves relationships and increases happiness. Gratitude makes life easier and is a powerful tool for success. It's no wonder so many people who are ungrateful find it so difficult to find moments of happiness and contentment. With practice, gratitude can become a regular part of your life.

There are a few techniques you can use to develop gratitude in your day-to-day life. One is to write down five or ten things you're grateful for each day. Another is to practice gratitude mindfulness meditation. Gratitude is something that can be developed and practiced in business and personal life. The key is to find moments of happiness and contentment, and to remember the feeling of gratitude for those moments.

Be grateful for everything you have been given.

Gratitude is one of the most important things you can do for yourself and for those around you. It can be easy to lose sight of the blessings you have been given when your life is going smoothly. Remember to practice gratitude in good times as well as bad and all the moments in the middle.

Not only should you be grateful for your possessions, but you should be grateful for the people in your life. Whether it's friends or family, you should be grateful for who you have been given and everything they mean to you. I recommend you also practice gratitude for the places that are precious to you: your home, your yard, your neighborhood, your favorite nature places ....

Gratitude will help you for the rest of your life.

4. HONESTY

When I was younger, I used to think that honesty was simply putting the truth out there. But now that I am older and know better, I realize that honesty is being true to yourself and being honest with others. It is being honest about your feelings and being true to your own desires. Honesty is important, and it makes the world a better place.

What is honesty? It is simply being true to yourself and your feelings. Honesty can be demanding, but it is important to the world. Everyone has different desires, and it is important to be true to what you want. Honesty can make the world better for all of us.

Honesty is important in both your business and personal life. It is the foundation of all healthy relationships, and it is an essential key to success. It is important to be honest with the people you work with and for, and those who work for you. Providing honest, constructive feedback will help you build and sustain harmonious, mutually beneficial working relationships.

Finally, it is important to be honest with yourself. When you start to develop a sense of honesty, you will also start to develop a better sense of character. One of the best ways to develop a good sense of honesty is to keep a journal. Writing down your thoughts, feelings, and experiences will help you develop your own honest self. So, while it is important to be honest in business and personal life, it is even more important to be honest with yourself. Without a good sense of honesty, you will not be able to achieve success.

5. TRUST

Trust is one of the most crucial factors for success in any business. It's what allows people to work together and share common goals. It's also what separates successful businesses from those that are not so successful.

There are a lot of ways to develop trust in your business. One way is to learn about trust-building techniques. The next way is to put them into practice.

Some of the most common trust-building techniques are:

1. Be transparent with your customers.
2. Let customers know what you expect from them.
3. Be honest with your customers.
4. Let customers know your goals for them.
5. Be willing to change your plans if the customer is not happy with them.
6. Take care of your customers.

Trust is one of the most important things a business can have. It allows customers to feel comfortable and to trusting you, which can result in more sales, more growth, and more loyalty from customers. In business, your reputation is the greatest currency of all, and that is built upon trust.

CHAPTER 22

The Joy of Living Is in Giving

The gift of living is not living for yourself but living for others you care about. When we give selflessly, we are given a chance to live bigger and better than we would otherwise.

It's easy to get wrapped up in our own lives and forget about the people around us. We can get so focused on our own needs and wants that we lose sight of what really matters. But when we take the time to think about others, and put their needs before our own, we find a whole new level of happiness and fulfillment.

When we focus on others, we find that we are happier and more content. We learn to appreciate and enjoy life more. And we come to see that the greatest happiness comes not from acquiring things for ourselves, but from helping people. This is the joy of living.

So, the next time you're feeling down or frustrated with life, try putting others first. Smile at a stranger, help someone carry their bags, or do something kind for a friend. You'll be surprised at how much better you feel afterward. The joy of living is in giving, and it's a feeling that is truly priceless.

When you give of yourself—your time, your talents, your love—it's the best feeling in the world. You're not thinking about yourself; you're thinking about someone else. This takes you out of your own negative thought pattern, dissolves fears and worries instantly, and brings a smile to both of your faces.

Giving is one of the most joyous and rewarding experiences in life.

THE ACT OF GIVING

It can be simply defined as the act of voluntarily transferring something of value to another person or organization. Whether it's donating your time, money, possessions, or skills, giving from the heart is a sure way to experience more joy and contentment.

There are many reasons why giving is such a wonderful way to live a joyful life. For one, giving is a way to make a real difference in the world. When you give your time, talents, or money to a worthy cause, you are helping to improve the lives of others. This can be incredibly fulfilling and make you feel like you are making a real difference in the world.

Another reason why giving is so joyful is because it is a way to connect with others. When you give to someone else, you build a connection with them. By sharing something that is important to you, you create a bond between you and the other person. It is a meaningful way to build strong relationships with the people around you.

Finally, giving is a way to experience joy in the moment. When you give of yourself, you can enjoy the moment and appreciate all that is good in your life. You are not focused on yourself, but on others and what you can do to help them. This is a wonderful way to connect with others and to feel a sense of purpose. When you are able to help others, you feel more happy and fulfilled.

HOW CAN I GIVE MY TIME TO OTHERS?

There are so many ways to give your time to others—even if you are already busy. Think about all the people in your life who could use a little help. Are there elderly neighbors who could use someone to run errands for them or cut their lawn? Are there busy mothers who could use a break for a few hours? Are there children who need someone to read to them or help with their homework? There are endless opportunities to give of your time, and you don't have to spend a lot of time or money to do so.

Sometimes, all it takes is a few minutes to make someone else's day a little bit brighter.

One of the best things about giving your time is that it often results in making new friends. When you take the time to get to know someone, you often find that you have a lot in common. You may also find that you have received far more than you have given. What better way to spend my time than helping others? It feels good to help others, and it makes you happy. There are so many things you can do to give time to others. You can volunteer, you can donate money or goods, or you can just be there for someone who needs a friend.

Just being there for someone who needs a friend is a wonderful way to give back. Sometimes all someone needs is someone to listen. Try offering support to someone who is going through a tough time.

This is the joy of living, to be able to give of ourselves to others. It is a way to connect with others and make a difference in their lives. When we give, we ourselves are also enriched. We feel good about ourselves because we have helped someone else.

Volunteering is a terrific way to give back to the community. There are many organizations that need volunteers, and there are many ways to help. You can volunteer at a homeless shelter, at a food bank, or at an animal shelter. You can do a litter cleanup at the river or park. You can also volunteer time at a charitable organization.

HERE ARE SOME OTHER WAYS YOU CAN GIVE:

Donating money or goods is another way to give back. Many organizations accept donations, and there are many ways to donate.

Donating money is one of the easiest and most common ways. You can donate to many different organizations, large or small, and your donation will be put to beneficial use. There are also many websites that allow you to donate money directly to a specific cause.

Donating clothes or household items is another terrific way to give back. There are many organizations that accept such, and they will often distribute the clothing to people in need. You can also donate clothes to people directly in your local community. Some churches will also accept donations to help the needy.

Donating food is a wonderful way to help those who are struggling. Some of the many organizations that accept donations of food will distribute the food to those who need it. You can also donate food to people in your local community.

Donating toys is a fantastic way to help children in need. There are many organizations that accept donations of toys or stuffed animals (please wash them first), and they will often distribute the toys to children who will enjoy them most. If there is a children's hospital in your area, they may also accept donations.

So be sure to include giving in your life. It is one of the greatest joys you will ever experience! It is also a way to connect with God. When we give, we are doing what God wants us to do. He loves it when we help others, and He blesses us for our kindness.

HOW DO I GIVE OF MY TALENTS TO OTHERS?

You can give your talent to others in many ways. You can share your knowledge and skills by teaching others. When you teach someone else what you know, you help them learn and grow. Not only do they gain new skills, but they also gain a better understanding of the world around them. One of the most rewarding things in life is to teach someone something new and see the look of amazement on their face when they grasp the concept you are teaching. It is also a great way to build new relationships and make new connections.

When I taught musical instruments to children, it was so gratifying to see the look of excitement on their faces when they finally mastered a new skill. Sharing your talent with others is a great way to make other people feel appreciated and special. And who knows? You might just inspire someone to pursue their own talents. If you have an ability or skill that you can share with others, consider teaching them. It's an extremely uplifting experience, and you may make some new friends in the process!

Another way to share your talent is by showing your abilities. When you show others what you can do, you help them understand your skills and talents. This can be a wonderful way to inspire others and help them achieve their own goals. Plus, it can be a lot of fun to share your skills with others and see them succeed.

Not only can you share your talents with others by showing your abilities, but you can also inspire them by sharing your story. When you share your story, you encourage others by showing them it is possible to achieve their goals. By sharing your story, you also help others understand what your journey has been like. And, finally, by sharing your story, you inspire others to follow their dreams. So, if you want to share your talent with the world, then show your abilities, share your story, and encourage others to follow their dreams. It's sure to be a rewarding experience for everyone involved.

Another way to share your talent is by contributing your time and effort in a coaching environment. Coaching others to achieve their goals not only allows you to share your talents, but it also allows you to make a real difference in someone's life.

When you dedicate yourself to helping others grow and succeed, you not only make the world a better place but also make yourself a better person in the process. If you are looking for a way to share your talents with the world, consider coaching others. It's a great way to make a difference, and it is sure to inspire others as well.

Writing a book can be another way to give your talents to others. Writing a book is a lot of work, but you may find it is well worth the effort. If you feel you have a great story to tell, or helpful hints on how to do anything better, in any subject, consider writing a book. This is a great way to give your talents to others. You can share your story with the world and help people learn and grow. You leave a legacy that lives on long after you are gone.

If you don't want to write a book, you could always share your talents in other ways. You could write a song, start a blog, or share on social media. Whatever you do, make sure you share your talents with others. You never know who might be inspired by what you have to say.

Whatever ways you find most helpful and joyful, remember that sharing your talent with others can make the world a better place. And you a better human.

CHAPTER 23

The Principle of Empowerment

To live a better life, you need to be empowered.

There's no question that empowerment is key to a happy and fulfilled life. But what does it mean to be empowered, exactly?

Empowerment means being able to fulfill your potential. It means having the ability to make choices that support your goals and dreams. It means being in control of your own life and having the power to create the future you want for yourself. It allows you to create your own reality and to be the architect of your own destiny. When you're empowered, you're not as susceptible to outside influences. You are not as easily swayed by others and not as likely to let fears or doubts hold you back. You're more likely to trust yourself and act on your own intuition.

Being empowered also means being willing to stand up for what you believe in, even when it's not popular or easy. It means being strong enough to face adversity and challenges and maintain the courage to stay true to yourself and your values—no matter what.

Ultimately, empowerment is about claiming your power and using it to create a life that you love. It's about stepping into your authentic self and becoming the master of your own destiny. When you're empowered, you're not a victim of your circumstances. You don't blame others for your problems or feel like you're at the mercy of fate. You take responsibility for your life, and you're in control of your own happiness. Being empowered helps you to grow and develop into the person you want to be. It allows you to tap into your inner resources and use them to create the life you want. Empowerment is about self-reliance and self-fulfillment. It is about becoming the best version of yourself.

When you are empowered, you feel strong and capable. You feel confident in your ability to make a difference in the world. You are not afraid to take risks and face challenges. You know that you can handle whatever comes your way. This gives you the courage to go after and ultimately live your dreams.

Empowerment is a powerful force for positive change. It enables you to do great things and make a difference in the world. When you are empowered, you can change the world for the better.

There are many things in the world that need to change. You can't sit back and wait for someone else to do it. You must take action and empower yourself to make a difference. It's not always easy, but it's worth it.

Think about the issues that are important to you. What can you do to make a difference? You might not be able to solve everything, but every little bit helps. You can start by spreading awareness and educating others.

It's important to stay hopeful and never give up. You can make a difference.

It's up to us to create the world we want to live in, but we must work together and support each other. Let's empower ourselves and make a difference!

HOW DO I EMPOWER MYSELF?

Some of the most important ways are by taking action, setting goals, and being yourself.

1. *Taking Action*

Taking action, especially when you are afraid, can help you grow as a person and achieve new things. Taking action can help you feel empowered and capable of achieving anything you set your mind to. Not being afraid to try new things can help you become a mature person.

Recently, I tried something new, and it made me feel really empowered. I was a little scared at first, but I did it anyway and it was a great experience. Sometimes it's good to push yourself out of your comfort zone and try something new. This can greatly improve your motivation to learn new things.

Empowerment doesn't mean that you have to do something wild or crazy. It can be as simple as trying a new food or taking on a new challenge at work. Whatever it is, just make sure it's something that interests you and that you're excited about.

Trying new things will help you become more confident in your abilities. When you take action, you're not afraid to put yourself out there. You'll be more likely to reach your goals and achieve success.

When you're empowered, you feel confident and in control. You know that you can handle whatever life throws your way. So, don't be afraid to try new things; it can be really rewarding!

2. Setting Goals

Setting goals helps you stay focused on what you want to achieve. It helps you stay motivated and make progress toward your goals. However, it's important to empower yourself along the way. This means believing in yourself, your abilities, and your worth. It means having the courage to take risks and make mistakes.

To empower yourself, you must set goals and believe in yourself. If you don't believe in yourself, no one else will. You need to have confidence in your abilities and your worth. Know that you can do whatever you put your mind to. Then remind yourself of your accomplishments and focus on your strengths. When you believe in yourself, you're more likely to take action and achieve your goals.

Another way to empower yourself is to do something that makes you feel good about yourself. Whether it's taking care of yourself mentally and emotionally or taking care of your appearance, doing something that brings you pleasure will help you feel more confident and empowered. Also, empower yourself by surrounding yourself with positive people. They will help to encourage and support you as you work toward your goals.

Finally, don't set yourself up for failure by setting unrealistic goals. Set goals that challenge you but are still attainable. Use the SMART goal formula all the time. When you achieve your goals, you'll feel more confident and empowered.

3. Being Yourself

Be true to yourself and embrace who you are—your strengths, your weaknesses, and everything in between. Get to know yourself. What makes you happy? What are your passions? What skills do you have? When you're yourself, you're not letting others control you. This can help you stay true to yourself and your values.

When you're empowered, you have the confidence to be yourself and to achieve anything you set your mind to. You're also more likely to be happy and content with who you are, which is a key ingredient in a happy and fulfilling life. So be yourself, embrace who you are, and go out and achieve anything you want in life!

HOW DO I EMPOWER OTHERS?

There is no single answer to this question, as empowering others will vary depending on the individual. However, there are some general things you can do to empower others.

First, listen to other people and take their concerns seriously. Too often, people are dismissed or ignored, which can make them feel powerless. You can empower others by giving them a voice. When someone feels like they're being heard and their concerns are being addressed, they feel empowered. Showing genuine concern and respect for others is the best way to empower them and help them feel like their opinion matters, their contribution has value, and they can make a difference.

Second, give them support and help them feel confident in themselves. This means giving them the space to make mistakes, providing encouragement, and being there to help them learn and grow. Nobody is perfect, and everyone makes mistakes. By empowering others, we help them feel confident enough in their abilities to learn from their mistakes and become better individuals. We all have something to offer, and by empowering others, we help them find their voice and share their gifts with the world. When you offer your support and encouragement to others, it gives them the boost they need.

Another way to empower others is to give them responsibility and authority. This can be done by delegating tasks or giving them decision-making authority. When people are given responsibility, they feel like they are a part of the team, and they can make a difference. They feel like they have control over their own lives.

Don't be afraid to give other people some freedom. Everyone is different, and they will not all want the same things. Allow them to make their own choices and make mistakes, and trust that they will learn from their experiences. This type of freedom can empower them to find their own path in life.

Finally, you can empower others by helping them to develop their own skills and abilities. When people feel like they can do things on their own, they feel more empowered. You can help them to develop their skills by providing training or coaching, or by giving them opportunities to try new things. When people feel like they can do things themselves, they feel more in control of their lives, and they feel more empowered.

WHY IS EMPOWERMENT IMPORTANT IN PURSUING A BETTER LIFE?

When it comes to bettering yourself, empowerment is key. When you are empowered, you are confident in your ability to make decisions and take action. When you feel empowered, you feel capable of directing your own life and creating the future you want for yourself. This is why empowerment is so important in pursuing a better life.

When you empower yourself, you open up possibilities that may have seemed out of reach. You can become more motivated and determined to achieve your goals, and you can better face the challenges that come your way. With empowerment comes a greater sense of control over your life. This can be incredibly empowering in and of itself.

So, if you want to achieve a better life, start by empowering yourself. Believe in yourself and believe that you have the power to create the life you want. With courage and determination, anything is possible.

When you feel empowered, you believe in yourself and your ability to achieve your goals. You have the courage and determination to pursue your dreams and make them a reality. Empowered individuals are also more likely to take action, which is essential for making progress.

CHAPTER 24

Leadership Is Action, Not Position

A leader is someone who takes action and gets things done. They are not defined by their position but by their ability to motivate and inspire others to act. This is what makes a great leader: someone who can not only take charge but also motivate and inspire others to do their best.

Keep in mind that you don't have to be in a leadership role to lead. Leadership is not a title; it is an approach to life. Anyone can lead, it just depends on what you're willing to do.

Leadership is not about being in charge, it's about making a difference. It's about affecting change and inspiring others to do the same. It's about creating a vision and leading people toward it.

WHAT ARE THE MISSIONS OF LEADERSHIP?

There are many different missions of leadership, but all share one common goal: the success of the organization or team. The key to success depends on the leader's ability to serve others, to make a difference, to inspire and motivate their team, to lead by example, to foster a culture of trust and collaboration, and to create a clear vision and shared purpose to guide their team toward success.

1. Serving others

This is a fundamental principle of leadership. Leaders exist to serve others. They put the needs of others before their own, and they work to help others achieve their goals. Leaders step up to help people achieve their goals and dreams. They provide support and guidance and help people reach their potential.

This mission is at the heart of everything a leader does. It drives their decisions and their actions. It inspires them to work hard and to make sacrifices. And it motivates them to serve others selflessly. When leaders focus on serving others, they create a positive impact in the world. They make a difference in the lives of those they lead. This is what makes leadership so important and so meaningful. Leadership is not about advancing oneself; it's about advancing others. It's not about taking control; it's about enabling others to succeed. It's not about making things happen; it's about helping others make things happen.

2. Making a difference

Leaders make a difference. Their mission is to affect positive change and make the world a better place. This is what leaders do and why we need them. Leaders exist to empower others to reach their potential and achieve their goals. It is about creating a culture of accountability where people are encouraged to take risks and think for themselves.

The mission of a leader is to use their skills and talents to help others achieve their goals, reach their potential, and make a positive impact on the world. Leaders strive to improve the lives of others and make the world a better place. They are dedicated to making a difference, and they never give up.

3. Inspiring others

Leaders are inspirational figures. They motivate others to achieve great things and encourage people to dream big and pursue their passions. It is the responsibility of the leader to motivate and inspire their followers to achieve common goals. A leader must be able to communicate effectively and be willing to put in the extra effort to get the job done. Leaders must also be able to make tough decisions and stay calm under pressure.

The ability to inspire others is one of the most important traits of a leader. When people are inspired, they are more motivated, creative, focused, and productive. A leader must be able to inspire others to want to achieve something greater. Leaders must also be willing to take risks and make sacrifices for the betterment of their team or organization. To be a successful leader, you must be able to put others first and always keep the mission of leadership in mind.

4. *Leading by example*

Leaders set the example for others to follow. They lead with integrity and honesty, and they strive to always do the right thing. It's what drives leaders to make the tough decisions, even when they know they might not be popular. It's what drives them to put their own interests aside and focus on the needs of their team. And it's what allows them to stay strong in the face of adversity.

Leaders understand that their actions have a ripple effect. They know that the decisions they make and the example they set can influence others in a positive or negative way. That's why they always aim to lead with integrity and honesty. They want to be someone their team can look up to and emulate.

Of course, leaders don't always get it right. But that's okay. They're human, and they're allowed to make mistakes. What's important is that they learn from their mistakes and continue to strive for excellence. However, it's not just about making mistakes. They need to be someone that others can look up to and admire. They need to be someone who is always willing to put in the extra effort, even when things get tough. Most importantly, a leader needs to be always willing to learn. No one is perfect, and leaders need to be open to constructive feedback from their team members. They also need to be willing to experiment and try new things. After all, innovation is key to success in any organization.

Leaders need to work hard every day to live up to their mission and set the example for others.

---

5. Fostering a culture of trust and collaboration

Leadership is not about individual achievement or making things happen through directives. Rather, it is about creating an environment where people feel safe to take risks and innovate. A key part of this is establishing a culture of trust, where people can openly share their ideas and opinions.

Leaders must also be willing to collaborate with their team rather than try to control everything themselves. By establishing trust and collaboration, leaders can create a productive and inspiring environment where teamwork thrives, and employees are more engaged. When employees feel that they can trust their leader, they are more likely to be open and forthcoming with their ideas. Likewise, when leaders collaborate with their team, employees feel appreciated and that their contributions are valued. Ultimately, this creates a more productive and positive work environment.

6. Creating a clear vision and shared purpose

In any workplace, it is important to have a clear sense of purpose and direction. This helps to create a sense of identity and common goals for everyone in the organization. It can help to motivate and inspire people to work together toward common goals.

A leader's mission is to create a vision for the organization and then motivate and guide employees to achieve that vision. This can be a challenging task, but it is essential for creating a productive and positive work environment.

Leaders must have the courage to take risks, the compassion to listen to others, and the wisdom to make decisions that will benefit the greatest number of people.

A clear vision gives people a sense of where the organization is going and what it stands for. It can provide a framework for making decisions and can help to guide the organization through tough times. A shared purpose helps to unite the organization and provides a common goal that everyone can work toward. It can help to build team spirit and encourage people to work together for the benefit of the organization.

WHY IS LEADERSHIP IMPORTANT IN PURSUING FOR A BETTER LIFE?

Leadership is important for many reasons, but chiefly because it enables you to effectively mobilize others toward a common goal. Leadership is something that can be learned and developed over time. It takes hard work and dedication, but it is worth it.

Being able to inspire and motivate people to achieve wonderful things is essential for creating a better life for everyone. Leaders are also able to make tough decisions when necessary and guide their followers through challenging times. In short, leadership is essential for achieving success both personally and professionally. Not only will leadership skills help you to achieve your goals, but they will also help you motivate other people to achieve great things.

For a group of people to achieve a common goal, there must be a leader to guide them. Leadership is important in pursuing a better life because it allows individuals to work together and achieve objectives that they may not be able to accomplish on their own. A leader can inspire others to reach their full potential. Furthermore, a leader can help create a sense of community and camaraderie, which can be beneficial in times of hardship.

Ultimately, leadership is important in pursuing for a better life because it allows individuals to come together and work toward a common goal.

Being a leader is not always easy, but it is definitely rewarding. When you become a leader, you are able to make a positive impact on the world and help others achieve their dreams. Leaders are also able to create change and make a difference in people's lives. So, if you want to make a difference in the world and pursue a better life for yourself and others, then leadership is definitely the way to go. Leadership is not easy, but it is worth the effort. So, go and make a difference!

CHAPTER 25

Your Abundant, Balanced, and Fulfilling Life

WHAT IS AN ABUNDANT LIFE, AND HOW CAN I ACHIEVE IT?

An abundant life is one that is full of happiness, love, and joy. It is a life where you have plenty of time to do the things that delight and uplift you, to be with the people you treasure most. It is a life where you feel deeply fulfilled in your day-to-day activities. You are successful in all areas of your life, including your relationships, your career, and your personal goals.

You can create an abundant life for yourself by following these simple steps:

1. Set your intentions.

Before you can achieve anything, you need to know what it is you want. Sit down and write out a list of your goals, both personal and professional. Be specific and be sure to include a timeframe for each goal. Better still, put your goals to the S.M.A.R.T. test.

2. Take action.

Once you have your goals in place, it's time to take action. This doesn't mean working eighteen hours a day; it means taking small steps each day, and larger leaps as needed, to move you closer to your goals.

3. Visualize your success.

Seeing yourself achieve your goals is the first step to making them a reality. Start by visualizing yourself living a successful, abundant life. Doing this on a regular basis will help to keep you motivated and focused on what you want to achieve. It will also help you feel the affirming emotions you associate with that success.

4. Stay positive.

When you focus on the good things you already have in your life, you'll be more likely to attract more good things. Positive thinking is a crucial key to creating an abundant life.

5. Believe in yourself.

The most important step of all is to believe in yourself. You need to know that you really do have the power to create the life you want and that you are capable of achieving anything you set your mind to.

WHAT IS A BALANCED LIFE AND HOW CAN I ACHIEVE IT?

In a balanced life, you have excellent work-life balance. A good work-life balance means that you have time for work and time for your personal life. Time for play, time for socializing, and time for resting. You should make sure that you are not working all the time and that you also are not spending excessive time on your personal life. You should have enough time for work, family, friends, and yourself—for relaxation and fun.

You also need to have a good balance between your time and your energy. You should not spend all your time doing things that use up a lot of energy. You should also not spend all your time doing things that do not use up any energy, for example, being a couch potato. It is an interesting paradox that when we exercise the right amount, we somehow gain energy!

A balanced life is important for your physical and mental health, which can help you be more productive and successful. You need to have good habits and routines to be successful.

Here are a few things you can do to achieve a balanced life:

- *Set priorities and stick to them.*
- *Make a schedule and stick to it.*
- *Say no to things you don't want to do.*
- *Find a hobby or activity that you enjoy and make time for it.*
- *De-stress by relaxing and spending time with friends and family.*
- *Reward yourself every time you accomplished a certain goal.*

WHAT IS A FULFILLING LIFE AND HOW CAN I ACHIEVE IT?

A fulfilling life is a life that is abundant, balanced, and successful. A fulfilling life is a life that you create for yourself. You create it by filling your life with positive things and by removing the negative things. You create a fulfilling life by living in harmony with yourself and with the world around you. You create a successful life by achieving your goals and dreams.

A fulfilling life has meaning and significance. It is a life that you are excited to live each day. A fulfilling life is a happy life. You can achieve this by living a life of purpose and passion. You need to find what makes you feel alive and excited—and do more of those things. You also need to find ways to balance your life so that you are not overly stressed or overwhelmed. And finally, you need to be successful in all areas of your life, including your relationships, career, and finances.

WHAT DOES LIVING A FULFILLING LIFE MEAN TO ME?

It's so important to find what you're passionate about and to put a great deal of your energy into pursuing it. Because when you're doing something you love, it's not really work at all. You'll be happy and fulfilled, and that's what leads to a successful life.

You also need to have a sense of purpose. Why are you doing what you're doing? What is your intention behind your actions? When you have a clear purpose, it's far easier to stay motivated and focused. You'll be more likely to achieve your goals and live a fulfilling life. Of course, it's not always easy to find your passion or purpose. It can take time and some experimentation, but it's worth the effort. When you find your passion and purpose, your life will change for the better. So don't give up. Keep looking until you find what you're looking for.

There are plenty of things you can do to make sure that you're living a rewarding life. But the most important thing is to find something that truly makes you happy. It could be a job, a hobby, a business, or anything else that you're passionate about. One of the best ways to find out what it is that you're passionate about is to try new things. Experiment with different careers, hobbies, and activities until you find something that really speaks to you. Don't be afraid to take risks—after all, the only way to find out if something is right for you is to try it out. Personally, I didn't even know that I could be passionate about writing until I started to write this book.

HOW DO I CREATE A FULFILLING AND SUCCESSFUL LIFE?

All of us have different ideas of what a fulfilling and successful life looks like. But there are a few key things that are common to most people's definition of a good life. Use these five tips to help you find fulfillment and achieve success in your life:

1. Define your goals and priorities.

Figure out what's important to you and what you want to achieve. Don't try to do everything at once. Focus on one or two key goals at a time and work toward them.

2. Take action.

Don't just sit around dreaming about, or even praying for, what you want. God helps those who help themselves. Take action and make it happen. Practice a "do it now" philosophy and never procrastinate. Don't wait for a perfect time to get started because there is not such thing. Take action now and work as hard as you can. The harder you work, the more successful you'll be.

3. Stay positive and motivated.

No one achieves success without a lot of challenging work and determination. Stay positive and motivated and keep pushing yourself to reach your goals. The best way to motivate yourself is to keep doing the work until you achieve what you want.

4. Persevere through setbacks.

There will be times when you'll stumble and fall. But it's important to pick yourself up and keep going. Persevere through setbacks and you'll eventually reach your goals. Remember that old saying about turning stumbling blocks into steppingstones?

5. Enjoy the journey.

Success is not a destination; it's a journey. Make sure you take the time to enjoy the journey, and don't focus solely on the end goal.

Keep working toward something larger than yourself, something that has meaning and purpose for you.

When you're young, it seems like there's so much time ahead of you to do whatever you want. You can pick any career, travel wherever you want, and date whomever you please. But as you get older, you realize that life is short, and you need to start figuring out what you want to do with it.

A fulfilling and successful life is not just about having a decent job and a loving family. It's about finding out what makes you happy and going after it. It's about being true to yourself and living your best life every day. So don't wait any longer. Start working toward your goals and dreams, and don't let anyone stop you. The world is your oyster!

This could be anything from making a difference in the larger world to simply helping others achieve their dreams. When you have both purpose and passion in your life, you will find that you are much more satisfied and happier regardless of what challenges come your way.

So, what are you doing to make your life more fulfilling and successful? Are you following your passions and working toward a larger purpose? If not, now is the time to start making some changes. The payoff will be well worth it!

Your journey to pursue a better life for yourself and for your family starts NOW.

CHAPTER 26

A.G.D.E.L. in Summary

ATTITUDE

To achieve a successful and abundant life, it is important to have the right attitude toward learning. Learning is not just about acquiring current information or skills but also about growing and developing as a person. To learn, we need to be willing to experiment, explore, and take risks. We also need to be prepared to face challenges and setbacks and learn from them.

The best way to learn is by doing and by making mistakes. We need to be willing to try new things, even if we don't know how they will turn out. We also need to be prepared to face challenges and setbacks and learn from them. When we are open to learning new things, we can grow and develop as individuals. This is the key to achieving success and happiness in life.

GOALS

There are many things we can do to achieve a better life but setting SMART (Specific, Measurable, Achievable, Relevant, Time-Bound) goals may be the most important. When we set clear, attainable goals, we increase our chances of success. Achieving our goals not only makes us feel good, but it also teaches us valuable life lessons.

There are a few key things to keep in mind when setting goals. First, make sure your goals are specific and measurable. This means you can track your progress and know when you've reached your goal. Second, make sure your goals are realistically achievable. Don't set yourself up for disappointment by aiming too high or too low.

Make sure your goals are relevant to your life. They should be important to you and something you're truly motivated to achieve. Finally, your goals need to be Time-Bound, attached to a certain timeframe for each outcome.

If you can keep these things in mind, setting and achieving goals will become easier and more satisfying. So, start thinking about what you want to achieve in life and get started on making it happen!

DETERMINATION

When it comes to success, many people believe that it's all about luck and opportunity. However, if you want to achieve remarkable things in life, you need to be determined and persistent. These two traits are essential in pursuing an abundant, balanced, fulfilling, and successful life.

Determination means that you're willing to do whatever it takes to achieve your goals, no matter how challenging things get. You have the drive and determination to keep going, even when times are tough.

Persistence means that you don't give up easily. You keep pushing forward no matter what obstacles get in your way. You know that success is within reach, and you're willing to do whatever it takes, within reason and your ethics, to get there.

Together, determination and persistence create a powerful force that can help you overcome any obstacle. These traits will help you stay focused on your goals and keep moving forward, no matter what challenges you face. So, if you want to achieve something, don't give up. Pursue it relentlessly, and you'll find success.

EXCELLENCE

To achieve an abundant, balanced, fulfilling, and successful life, you must aim for excellence. To do something well is to enjoy it. Excellence is a key factor in pursuing a better life.

This book provides a framework for achieving levels of excellence in every area of life. It teaches you how to set and achieve goals, develop better relationships, increase productivity and creativity, and overcome adversity. Achieving excellence is not easy, but it is worth the effort. The rewards of excellence are many and can include a fulfilling and successful life.

LEADERSHIP

Leadership is about serving others and making a difference in the world. It's about doing the right thing—even when no one is looking. It's about stepping up when others are stepping back. It's about making a difference, not making a fortune. True leaders are servants at heart, and they understand that the key to success is helping others achieve their goals.

Some people are born with natural leadership abilities, but for most people, leadership is learned. However, leadership is not about position; it's about influence.

Leadership is not a rank; it is an approach to life. A true leader inspires people to achieve more than they ever thought possible. A true leader builds relationships of trust and respect.

People often ask: How do I become a leader? The answer is you don't become a leader; you already are one. The challenge for most people is how to become a *great* leader.

FINAL THOUGHTS

In your pursuit of a better life, you first need to know what that means for you. What are your personal goals and aspirations? What do you want to achieve in your life? What makes you happy? Once you know what you want, you can begin taking steps toward achieving it.

One of the most important things to remember is that there is no one-size-fits-all approach to a better life. What works for someone else may not work for you, and that's okay. You need to find what makes you happy and go after it. This may require some experimentation and trial and error.

Another thing to keep in mind is that a better life is not something that happens overnight. It takes time and effort to achieve it. You need to be patient and stay focused on your goals. Don't get discouraged if things don't go perfectly according to plan. Just keep working toward your goals and don't give up.

The most important thing is to stay positive and believe in yourself. Pursuing a better life can be challenging, but it's definitely worth it. So don't hesitate any longer; get started on your journey today!

About the Author

Benjamin M. Noynay is a Filipino who migrated to Australia to pursue a better life for himself and for his family. Brother Ben, as he is fondly called by his seminary colleagues, graduated class valedictorian and holds a Bachelor of Arts Degree major in Philosophy and English from San Carlos Seminary College Cebu, in the Philippines.

While at school, Ben was appointed Assistant Music Director which helped him launch his musical career. Under the tutelage of Msgr. Rodolfo Villanueva, Ben learned how to train different types of choral groups. He was a sought-after choir trainer and director of many private and government establishments, schools, and corporate organizations.

In the Philippines, Ben worked as a university teacher, radio broadcaster, musical director, marketing manager, and insurance salesman. In Australia, he also worked at various jobs and started different businesses to support his family. In his pursuit of a better life, Ben becomes a business coach and continues to teach music.

At present, Ben runs his own coaching business under his own brand, RIGHT Coaching Systems. He also teaches piano, guitar, drums, bass, singing, songwriting and music production at his home music studio. Ben lives happily in Keysborough, Victoria with his beautiful and loving wife, giving thanks every day for blessing him with three successful children and two (so far), adorable granddaughters.

www.ingramcontent.com/pod-product-compliance
Lightning Source LLC
Chambersburg PA
CBHW050309010526
44107CB00055B/2171